SPIRIT OF LIGHT OR DARKNESS?

JULES J. TONER, S.J.

SPIRIT OF LIGHT OR DARKNESS?

*A Casebook for Studying
Discernment of Spirits*

THE INSTITUTE OF JESUIT SOURCES
1995

Number 11 in Series 3: Original Studies Composed in English

© The Institute of Jesuit Sources
3700 West Pine Boulevard
Saint Louis, MO 63108
Tel: [314] 977-7257
Fax: [314] 977-7263

Library of Congress Catalogue Card Number 95-77483
ISBN 1-880810-12-3

CONTENTS

✤   ONE   ✤

INTRODUCTION

Reviewers of *A Commentary on St. Ignatius' Rules for Discernment of Spirits* (hereafter referred to as *Commentary*)[1] and *Discerning God's Will* (hereafter referred to as *DGW*)[2] observed that more plentiful illustrations were needed. This casebook on discernment of spirits and a projected one on discerning God's will are intended, among other things, to remedy what was thought to be lacking in those earlier volumes. The cases presented in these books, along with the answers to the study questions, supply abundant illustration of the spiritual movements with which the Ignatian rules for the discernment of spirits are concerned, and also supply plentiful instances of the Ignatian times and modes for seeking God's will.

Main Purpose

To provide illustration, however, is neither the only nor the main purpose of these casebooks. In order to use them most effectively, the reader must understand and adhere to the main purpose and the prerequisites for achieving it. The main purpose of the earlier volume on discernment of spirits was to establish as accurately and clearly as I could the authentic teaching of St. Ignatius. The direct and primary purpose of this casebook assumes some at least initial understanding of that teaching and intends to provide a tool to assist the reader to grow in the ability to apply Ignatian principles and directives to experience, that is, to become increasingly adept at *doing* Ignatian discernment of spirits and discernment of God's will. The concomitant indirect but equally important purpose is, through presenting and analyzing cases, to bring the reader to a more penetrating, more exact, more clear, and more subtle understanding of Ignatian principles and directives.

---

[1] Jules Toner, *A Commentary on Saint Ignatius' Rules for the Discernment of Spirits* (St. Louis: The Institute of Jesuit Sources, 1982).

[2] Jules Toner, *Discerning God's Will: Ignatius of Loyola's Teaching on Christian Decision Making* (St. Louis: Institute of Jesuit Sources, 1991).

Even those who already have some sound learning regarding discernment of spirits and God's will as well as considerable experience in practice may also find these books useful for tuning up their skills and possibly for bringing them into contact with a different understanding of Ignatian principles and a different way of applying them.

Those who wish to engage in regular discussions on spiritual discernment, comparable to staff meetings in hospitals or clinics, might find another use for this volume. (The value of this kind of group study can hardly be overestimated.) Such persons can find in these books material to get their meetings under way or to see them through when the members do not come up with useful cases. They might also find in the procedure and method provided here some help for conducting their study before and during these meetings.

The questions for reflection on the cases and the proposed responses are not meant to teach how to practice spiritual direction except as it involves discernment of spirits and the counsels Ignatius includes in his directions for such discernment. Those who use these books may find that it suits their purpose to go beyond those limits, but the questions and responses are not of much help for doing this. Consequently, the proposed responses to the questions for reflection given with each case are not necessarily meant to indicate what a spiritual director should tell the directee in every such case. They might only serve as help for the director to understand how the rules for discernment of spirits apply in such cases. How this understanding is to be employed by the director is something that only the director can wisely decide in the concrete situation.[3]

Presuppositions

Presupposed for the effective use of this casebook in order to achieve the purpose stated above are awareness of and attention to one's own spiritual movements (thoughts, feelings, affective acts, decisions, and choices) over an extended period of time, along with some at least initial sound understanding of Ignatian teaching on discernment of spirits and of God's will. For the study of cases cannot be carried on fruitfully by those who do not lead an examined life, who have little or no reflective awareness of their own inner lives, or who have no familiarity with the spiritual teaching employed here for theoretical and practical understanding of the spiritual life. It is true that cases can be

---

[3] Some models of how the Ignatian rules can be integrated into spiritual direction may be found in Maureen Conroy, R.S.M., *The Discerning Heart* (Chicago: Loyola University Press, 1993).

used as a starting point in writing for or lecturing to those who have as yet little or no knowledge of spiritual discernment and who might have no more than an academic interest in the subject. The reader or listener could pick up some knowledge of what spiritual discernment is about; but this knowledge is not calculated to develop skill in actually doing such discernment.

Furthermore, since the solution of cases is done here in terms of the interpretation of Ignatius's writings presented in my *Commentary* (referred to above), some knowledge of what is in that book is, if not necessary, at least considerably advantageous for a fruitful study of cases. If readers do not already possess such knowledge, they can develop it while using this casebook in the method that will be presented below. The section "Explanatory Notes" in the casebook on discernment of spirits provides a condensed statement of the fundamentals developed more fully in *A Commentary on St. Ignatius' Rules for Discernment of Spirits*. The abbreviated statement, if carefully studied, will make it possible for readers to achieve the purpose of this casebook even though they have not read the book on which the condensed statement is based. The experience of many in discernment workshops and academic courses has shown that this is so. It has also shown that a study of the fuller treatment in the earlier book is notably more helpful than the condensations.

Some of the cases in this volume on discerning spirits involve a choice to be made, for which a discernment of God's will is required. In this volume the latter kind of discernment is left aside and attention limited to discernment of spirits. In the following volume, on cases for the study of discerning God's will, most of the cases will involve discernment of spirits as a way of finding God's will. It will, then, be helpful if the study of cases on discerning God's will is taken up after the study of cases on discerning spirits.

Source of Cases

Some cases were found in books, journals, or newspapers; some were constructed for teaching purposes; many, if not most, of the cases were given to me by students in theology classes or workshops and are accounts of actual experiences or, at least, adaptations of actual experiences, all used with permission. Whenever called for, the names of persons in the cases and at times the circumstances are changed in order to protect anonymity. Otherwise, with some editorial revisions for the sake of clarity or to fit the purpose of this book, the cases have been preserved in the words of those who contributed them and in the form they gave them. The paragraph numbers are added for the sake of easy reference in the questions for reflection and the answers to these.

I am responsible for the material contained in "Questions for Reflection" and for that found in "Proposed Responses." As step 4 of "Method for Studying Cases" will make clear, the proposed responses are just that: they are not presented as in every instance the only possible way of interpreting the cases. They should, therefore, be read critically as well as with care to understand them and evaluate them with an open mind. Sometimes different readings of the case can call for different responses to the questions. That is why discussion is so valuable in this kind of study.

Some readers will, as I do, regret the absence of cases to cover certain kinds of experiences. However, the aim of this book is not to cover every kind of case that might come up, but only enough to achieve the main twofold purpose indicated above. The cases given here seem varied enough for that purpose. If some readers are bothered because a disproportionate number of the cases concern women, I offer this simple explanation: Women have been more cooperative than have men in responding to my request for cases to use in my teaching and writing—and also because, at least in my teaching experience, more women than men seem to be interested in learning how to do spiritual discernment.

TWO

THE TEXT OF THE IGNATIAN RULES FOR THE DISCERNMENT OF SPIRITS

In order that those who are studying Ignatian teaching on discernment of spirits may have at hand the document which is central and foundational to such study, we present here a translation of the Rules for Discernment of Spirits, as found in *Spiritual Exercises*, [313–36].[1]

If it is true that every translation is an interpretation, it still seems clear that a free, rhetorically graceful translation of Ignatius's pedestrian and even awkward style of writing is likely to be much more an interpretation than a carefully literal one. There is, therefore, a greater chance of failing to convey the precise meaning of the original. For that reason, the translation presented here is painstakingly literal. Whatever explanation I think necessary is given in my *Commentary* on the rules and in the section "Explanatory Notes" given below. In this way, the reader has a translation as near to Ignatius's own words as I can make it and, by appeal to it, can critically evaluate my interpretation or explanation of each rule.

[Set I]

[313]   RULES TO HELP PERSONS GET IN TOUCH WITH AND UNDERSTAND IN SOME MANNER THE DIVERSE MOTIONS THAT ARE PROMPTED IN THEM, SO THAT THEY MAY RECEIVE THE GOOD ONES AND EXPEL THE EVIL ONES. THESE RULES ARE MORE APPROPRIATE TO THE FIRST WEEK [of the Spiritual Exercises].

[314]   Rule 1. In the case of those persons who go from mortal sin to mortal sin, the customary tactic of the enemy is to put before them illusory gratifications, prompting them to imagine sensual delights and pleasures, the better to hold them and make them grow in their vices and sins. With such persons, the good spirit employs a contrary tactic, through their rational power of moral judgment causing pain and remorse in their consciences.

[315]   Rule 2. As for those persons who are intensely concerned with purging away their sins and ascending from good to better in

---

[1] This translation is from Toner, *Commentary*, 24–30.

the service of God our Lord, the mode of acting on them is contrary to that [described] in the first rule. For then it is connatural to the evil spirit to gnaw at them, to sadden them, to thrust obstacles in their way, disquieting them with false reasons for the sake of impeding progress. It is connatural to the good spirit to give courage and active energy, consolations, tears, inspirations, and a quiet mind, giving ease of action and taking away obstacles for the sake of progress in doing good.

[316]   Rule 3. Concerning spiritual consolation. I name it [spiritual] consolation when some inner motion is prompted in the person of such a kind that he begins to be aflame with love of his Creator and Lord, and, consequently, when he cannot love any created thing on the face of the earth in itself but only in the Creator of them all. Likewise [I call it consolation] when a person pours out tears moving to love of his Lord, whether it be for sorrow over his sins, or over the passion of Christ our Lord, or over other things directly ordered to his service and praise. Finally, I call [spiritual] consolation every increase of hope, faith, and charity, and every inward gladness that calls and attracts to heavenly things and to one's personal salvation, bringing repose and peace in his Creator and Lord.

[317]   Rule 4. Concerning spiritual desolation. I call [spiritual] desolation everything the contrary of [what is described in] the third rule, for example, gloominess of soul, confusion, a movement to contemptible and earthly things, disquiet from various commotions and temptations, [all this] tending toward distrust, without hope, without love; finding oneself thoroughly indolent, tepid, sad, and as if separated from one's Creator and Lord. For just as [spiritual] consolation is contrary to [spiritual] desolation, in the same way the thoughts that spring from [spiritual] consolation are contrary to the thoughts that spring from [spiritual] desolation.

[318]   Rule 5. The time of [spiritual] desolation is no time at all to change purposes and decisions with which one was content the day before such desolation, or the decision with which one was content during the previous consolation. It is, rather, a time to remain firm and constant in these. For just as in [spiritual] consolation the good spirit generally leads and counsels us, so in [spiritual] desolation does the evil spirit. By the latter's counsels we cannot find the way to a right decision.

[319]   Rule 6. Granted that in [spiritual] desolation we ought not to change our previous purposes, it helps greatly to change ourselves intensely in ways contrary to the aforesaid desolation, for instance, by insisting more on prayer, on meditation, on much examination, and on extending ourselves to do penance in some fitting manner.

[320]   Rule 7. Let one who is in [spiritual] desolation consider how the Lord has left him to his natural powers, so that he may prove himself while resisting the disturbances and temptations of the enemy. He is, indeed, able to do so with the divine aid, which always remains with him even though he does not clearly perceive it. For, although the Lord has withdrawn from him his bubbling ardor, surging love, and intense grace, nevertheless, he leaves enough grace to go on toward eternal salvation.

[321]   Rule 8. Let him who is in [spiritual] desolation work at holding on in patience, which goes contrary to the harassments that come on him; and, while taking unremitting action against such desolation, as said in the sixth rule, let him keep in mind that he will soon be consoled.

[322]   Rule 9. There are three principal causes that explain why we find ourselves [spiritually] desolate. The first is that we are tepid, indolent, or negligent in our spiritual exercises; and, as a result of our own failings, [spiritual] consolation departs from us. The second is that it serves to put our worth to the test, showing how much we will extend ourselves in serving and praising God without so much pay in consolations and increased graces. The third is this: Spiritual desolation serves to give us a true recognition and understanding, grounding an inward experiential perception, of the fact that we cannot ourselves attain to or maintain surging devotion, intense love, tears, or any other spiritual consolation, but rather that all is gift and grace from God our Lord. So, we do not build a nest on another's property, elevating our mind in a certain pride or vainglory, giving ourselves credit for devotion or other constituents of spiritual consolation.

[323]   Rule 10. Let him who is in [spiritual] consolation think how he will bear himself in the [spiritual] desolation which will follow, gathering energy anew for that time.

[324]   Rule 11. Let him who is [spiritually] consoled set about humbling and lowering himself as much as he can, reflecting on how pusillanimous he is in the time of [spiritual] desolation without God's grace or consolation. On the other hand, let him who is in [spiritual] desolation keep in mind that, drawing strength from his Creator and Lord, he has with divine grace sufficiently great power to resist all his enemies.

[325]   Rule 12. The enemy acts like a shrewish woman, being weak and willful; for it is connatural to such a woman in a quarrel with some man to back off when he boldly confronts her; and on the contrary when, losing courage, he begins to retreat, the anger, vengeance, and ferocity of the woman swell beyond measure. In like man-

ner, it is connatural to the enemy to fall back and lose courage, with his temptations fading out, when the person performing spiritual exercises presents a bold front against the temptations of the enemy, by doing what is diametrically the opposite. If, on the contrary, the person engaged in spiritual exercises begins to be fearful and to lose courage while suffering temptations, there is no beast on the face of the earth so fierce as is the enemy of human kind in prosecuting his wicked intention with such swelling malice.

[326]   Rule 13. Likewise he behaves as a seducer in seeking to carry on a clandestine affair and not be exposed. When such a frivolous fellow makes dishonorable advances to the daughter of a good father or the wife of a good husband, he wants his words and seductions to be secret. On the contrary, he is greatly displeased when the daughter discovers to her father or the wife to her husband his fraudulent talk and lewd design; for he readily gathers that he will not be able to carry out the undertaking he has initiated. In like manner, when the enemy of human kind insinuates into the faithful person his wiles and seductions, he intensely desires that they be received in secret and kept secret. It dispirits him greatly when one discloses them to a good confessor or to another spiritual person who is acquainted with his trickery and malice; for when his evident trickery is brought to light, he gets the idea that he will not be able to realize the evil plan he has set in motion.

[327]   Rule 14. So also, in order to conquer and plunder what he desires, the enemy of human kind acts like a caudillo. For, just as a military commander in chief, pitching camp and exploring what the forces of a stronghold are and how they are disposed, attacks the weaker side, in like manner, the enemy of human kind roves around and makes a tour of inspection of all our virtues, theological and cardinal and moral. Where he finds us weaker and more in need of reinforcement for the sake of our eternal salvation, there he attacks us and strives to take us by storm.

[Set II]

[328]   RULES FOR THE SAME PURPOSE [as the first set], WITH MORE ACCURATE WAYS OF DISCERNING SPIRITS. THESE RULES ARE MORE SUITED FOR USE IN THE SECOND WEEK [of the Spiritual Exercises]

[329]   Rule 1. It is connatural for God and his angels, when they prompt interior motions, to give genuine gladness and spiritual joy, eliminating all sadness and confusion which the enemy brings on. It is connatural for the latter to fight against such gladness and spiritual

consolation by proposing specious arguments, subtle and persistently fallacious.

[330]   Rule 2. To give a person [spiritual] consolation without preceding cause is for God our Lord alone to do; for it is distinctive of the Creator in relation to the created person to come in and to leave, to move the person interiorly, drawing him or her totally into love of his Divine Majesty. I say without [preceding][2] cause, that is, without any previous perception or understanding of any object such that through it consolation of this sort would come by the mediation of the person's own acts of understanding and will.

[331]   Rule 3. With a [preceding] cause,[3] an angel, good or evil, can [spiritually] console a person. In doing so, the good and evil angels have contrary purposes. The purpose of the good angel is the person's progress, that he may ascend from good to better. The purpose of the evil angel is the contrary—and thereafter, to draw the person on to his damned intent and cunning trap.

[332]   Rule 4. It is characteristic of the evil spirit to take on the appearance of an angel of light, so that he can begin by going the way of a devout person and end with that person going his own [the spirit's] way. By that I mean that he first prompts thoughts which are good and holy, harmonious with such a faithful person, and then manages, little by little, to step out of his act and lead the person to his hidden falsehoods and perverse designs.

[333]   Rule 5. We ought to pay close attention to the progression of thoughts. If the beginning, middle, and end of it are altogether good and tend entirely to what is right, that is a sign of the good angel's influence. It is, however, a clear sign that the line of thought originates from the influence of the evil spirit, the enemy of our spiritual progress and eternal salvation, if the thoughts which he prompts end up in something evil or distracting or less good than what the person had previously proposed to do, or if they weaken, disquiet, or confuse him, doing away with the peace, tranquility, and quiet experienced beforehand.

[334]   Rule 6. When the enemy of human nature has been perceived and recognized by his telltale train of thoughts terminating in

---

[2] The phrase "without cause" has resulted in misunderstanding of an already unclear text. The phrase is certainly a contraction of "without preceding cause." Note that immediately following the contracted form, Ignatius writes, "I say without cause, *that is,* without any *previous perception* . . ." (emphasis mine). This explanatory clause also serves to make clear what sort of cause Ignatius intends to exclude from the experience he is describing.

[3] See note 5 above.

the evil to which he leads, it is useful for the person who was tempted by him to look immediately at the course of good thoughts that were prompted in him, noting how they began and how, little by little, the evil spirit contrived to make him fall away from the earlier sweetness and spiritual joy until he led him to what his [the spirit's] own corrupt mind intended. The purpose is that observing such an experience and taking mental note of it will be a safeguard for the future against these customary hoaxes of the evil spirit.

[335] Rule 7. Persons who are going from good to better the good angel touches sweetly, lightly, gently, as when a drop of water soaks into a sponge, while the evil spirit touches them sharply, with noise and disturbance, as when the drop of water falls on a rock. Those who are going from bad to worse the aforesaid spirits touch in a way contrary to the way they touch those going from good to better. The cause of this contrariety is that the disposition of the one touched is either contrary to or concordant with each of the said angels. For when it is contrary, the angels enter perceptibly, with clamor and observable signs; when it is concordant, they come in quietly, as one comes into his own house through an open door.

[336] Rule 8. Granted that when [spiritual] consolation is without [preceding] cause, it has no deception in it, since, as has been said, such consolation is from God our Lord alone; nevertheless, a spiritual person to whom God gives such consolation should, with great alertness and attention, examine his experience to discern the precise time of the actual consolation [without preceding cause] as distinct from the following time, in which the person is still glowing and still graced by the residue of [actual] consolation that is now over with. The reason for making this distinction is that frequently in this second period, either through one's own reasoning about the relations of concepts and judgments and the conclusions to be drawn from them, or through the influence of a good spirit or of an evil spirit, various purposes and opinions take shape that are not given immediately by God our Lord. Inasmuch as that is the case, these purposes and opinions are in need of prolonged and careful examination before full assent is given to them or they are put into execution.

THREE

EXPLANATORY NOTES ON THE IGNATIAN RULES FOR DISCERNMENT OF SPIRITS

PRELIMINARY CLARIFICATIONS

Discernment of Spirits Distinguished from Other Forms of Discernment (*Commentary,* 10–15)

There are manifold kinds of spiritual discernment: discernment of true and false doctrine, of true and false prophecy, of true and false mystical experiences and of different degrees or stages of mystical experience, discernment of what is truly God's will for one's free choice among alternative courses of action, to name only a few. The discernment we are interested in can be of service in all of these, but is not the same as any of them. Discernment of spirits is discernment among the inner movements of our minds and hearts to find and to interpret those that arise under the prompting of the Holy Spirit or the prompting of some spirit in opposition to the Holy Spirit or without the prompting of either of these.

The Meaning of "Spirits" (*Commentary,* 30–36)

What is meant by "spirits" in this context? By that term we refer to the Holy Spirit and to created spiritual beings (angels, Satan, and demons). There are some who question the reality of created spiritual beings. (What does Christian revelation have to say about them? For a response to this question, see *Commentary,* 36, 260–70.) Ignatius without doubt was sure of their reality, and we will speak from his point of view. But is there any reason for us to concern ourselves with any spirit other than the Holy Spirit? With the good angels, no; for whatever way they would influence us would be what the Holy Spirit wants them to do. About evil spirits, however, we need to concern ourselves very much. Most of the rules are taken up with discerning when the evil spirit is acting upon us and how to defeat him. In the context of our study, the term "evil spirit" will be extended to include not only evil spirits in the proper sense of the term, that is, created personal immaterial beings, but also the dispositions of evil within ourselves, the evil structures of society, all that can be a source of inner movements (of thoughts, affective feelings, and affective acts) contrary to what the Holy Spirit wishes to work in our lives through faith, love, and hope. The term will not include in its meaning those antispiritual movements themselves. Some commentators seem to understand evil spirit to mean such movements; they seriously misrepresent Ignatius's thought by doing so.

Purpose of This Study

Our purpose is not to get a theoretical theological understanding of discernment of spirits, except insofar as such understanding is needed for sound practice. Our purpose is, rather, to arrive at a deeper, clearer, more precise and accurate practical understanding of the Ignatian Rules for Discernment of Spirits, an understanding that will enable us to use them in our own lives and, if called to do so, in helping others.

INTRODUCTION TO THE IGNATIAN RULES FOR DISCERNMENT OF SPIRITS

Analysis of [313] (*Commentary*, 37–44)

There are two main topics that concern us in this introductory heading: the subject matter of the rules and the threefold purpose of the rules.

The Subject Matter: "Diverse Motions That Are Prompted in Them"

What are these "diverse motions"? They include thoughts (for example, judgments about God, self, the world; lines of reasoning; associations; fantasies; plans; and the like); affective acts (for instance, love, hate, desire, fear, hope); and affective feelings (for example, peace, confusion, warmth, coldness, sweetness, bitterness, dryness, buoyancy, heaviness, depression, and so on). In these rules, as we shall see, Ignatius is not interested in all the motions that we experience but only in those that of themselves tend to positively or negatively influence faith life (faith, hope, charity, prayer, religious ministry, and the like).

What does Ignatius mean by motions "that are prompted in them"? All these movements arise from the person in response to a situation as the person experiences it, with the persons, things, and events involved; but they are sometimes (often, in Ignatius's view) prompted by some personal spiritual agent, good or evil.

The Threefold Purpose of the Rules

The purpose of these rules, according to Ignatius, is to help persons get in touch with these motions, to understand them in some manner, and to receive or expel them. The first of these purposes, to get in touch with the motions, is prerequisite for the possibility of discerning spirits. The second constitutes discernment of spirits. The third is the reason for the first and the second: We want to understand these motions in order to receive or expel them. Let us comment on each of these purposes.

To get in touch with these motions means to become reflectively and discriminatingly aware of them. To do this is a relatively rare and difficult achievement. We are directly conscious of our inner experiences but rarely reflect on and evaluate them thematically. Even when we do, the motions are so manifold and fluid and complexly related that we do not readily discriminate among them. So, for most people, it takes long practice to be able to do it. One has to be patient with beginners, oneself or others. It will come with persevering effort and, above all, with enlightenment from the Holy Spirit.

To understand a motion once we are in touch with it means at least three things: (1) discerning the characteristic features by which it is distinguished from other motions; (2) discerning its direction, what consequences it tends to effect in one's own or another's spiritual life; (3) discerning its origin, what spirit is prompting this motion. Ignatius says that these rules are of value for understanding "in some manner" the motions within us. He is aware that they are not fully adequate for the purpose, that light from other sources is also needed.

To receive a motion means to let it work without hindrance, even to cooperate with it. To expel a motion means to oppose it, to strive to replace it with other motions, to refuse to act in accord with any tendency that it may occasion. It does not suggest that these motions can be ended by some direct violent effort. To expel does not mean to deny and repress the resisted motion. Neither does it mean that everything in the experience is necessarily evil; some element in it might be basically good and only needs redirection, reordering, purification.

The Mode of Referring to Individual Rules

The rules are divided into two distinct sets. The first set will be indicated by the Roman numeral *I* and the second by Roman numeral *II*. The rules in each set will be indicated by Arabic numbers. Thus, for example, the third rule in the first set will be referred to as I, 3, the seventh rule of the second set as II, 7.

RULES I, 1–2

The Most Fundamental Rules

As noted above, rules I, 1–4, are the fundamental rules of discernment of spirits; but among these, rules 1 and 2 are the most fundamental. Even rules 3 and 4 presuppose rules 1 and 2 for their significance in discerning spirits: they are a development, a further explanation, of rule 2. Without understanding the first two rules, the reader cannot fully understand anything in the Ignatian rules. Rule II, 7, illuminates rules I, 1–4 (*Commentary*, 53, 237–42).

Rules 1 and 2 throw light on each other and need to be studied together. They deal with contrary experiences; therefore, whatever is said about one implies something about the other (*Commentary*, 48f.).

These two rules deal with two contrary kinds of persons and the contrary effects, motions, prompted by the good and evil spirits in each of them. Just as the persons are contrary kinds, so also the motions prompted by the good and evil spirits in the two kinds of persons are exactly contrary.

Contrary Kinds of Persons (*Commentary*, 49–54)

The person in rule 1 is a spiritually regressing person, one who "goes from mortal sin to mortal sin." The meaning of "mortal sin" is uncertain in this rule. In any case, the significant factor is not the gravity of the sins but the direction of the person's life (from sin to sin), the developing dispositions underlying these sinful acts. If this interpretation is correct, Ignatius is not talking only about what we call "great sinners" but also about persons who in their present state could be considered rather good persons, who, however, have some growing egoistic disposition that is manifested in repeated selfish acts of one sort or another; this disposition constitutes a barrier to union with God and neighbor and causes one little by little to drift away from God.

The person in rule 2 is just the contrary of the person in rule 1. This person is spiritually maturing, one who is "going from good to better," turning from sin and growing in faith, hope, and charity. Again, the significant factor is not the person's measure of holiness but the direction of development in spiritual life, the kind of developing dispositions being established by and expressed in acts. Such a person is not necessarily very holy. He or she may even be someone who has just recently repented a very sinful life and who, with occasional failures, is spiritually maturing.

Contrary Kinds of Motions (*Commentary,* 54–60)

Now look at the motions prompted in these two persons, first of all those the evil spirit prompts in a spiritually regressive person. The direction of this person's life is the direction that the evil spirit intends. Therefore there is no clash between the evil spirit and this person when the former touches upon the person's regressive affective disposition. The spirit tries to keep the person moving in the direction his life has already taken. Ignatius says that the evil spirit commonly proposes "sensual delights." But not always in every person—unless we take this term in a broader meaning, something like St. Paul's use of the term "carnal." However the evil spirit does it, his main objective is to keep the regression going, to encourage, to "console," the person in that way of life.

The motions prompted by the Holy Spirit in this spiritually regressing person are altogether the contrary of what the evil spirit prompts (I, 1; II, 7). The Holy Spirit's intention goes against the direction of the person's life, trying to turn him around, cause a conversion. Therefore there is a clash. The Holy Spirit appeals to reason, conscience, causing pain and remorse. He appeals to all the good inclinations that remain in the regressing person—ultimately to the natural desire in every person for goodness, for truth, for God.

Now turn to the spiritually maturing person (I, 2). The motions prompted in this person by the good or evil spirits are just the contrary of those prompted by them in the spiritually regressing person. In the spiritually maturing person, the intent of the evil spirit clashes with the direction of this person's life and causes feelings of pain, sadness, confusion, and so forth. (For a fuller account, see the treatment of rule I, 4.) All this he does in order to discourage the person from going on from good to better. On the contrary, the Holy Spirit's influence merges with the disposition and direction of the person's life and causes positive motions, such as courage and energy to continue striving, peace and joy in doing so (see rule I, 3). For a treatment of the primary importance of "courage and energy," see *Commentary,* 63–69; and for two other basically important effects of the Holy Spirit that are not mentioned in rule 2 but are implied throughout the rules, see *Commentary, 69f.*

An important practical conclusion follows from the first two rules; namely, that anyone undertaking discernment of spirits had better be aware of which kind of person is experiencing the motions with which the discernment is concerned and which kind of disposition in the person is being touched on. A mistake about either of these facts will entail a misinterpretation of all these motions.

Concrete Complexities (*Commentary,* 70–78)

Unless we take account of the complexities in concrete experience (as opposed to pure cases), we will surely make mistakes in applying rules 1 and 2. In these rules Ignatius states pure cases, disengaged from the confusing complexities of concrete experience. It is a wise teaching method to do so in order to help us first grasp the basic concepts and principles of discerning spirits, without which the concrete complexities cannot be unraveled and understood. Now it is time to note some of these complexities.

1.   There is the similarity of spiritual and nonspiritual movements and their interweaving in experience. Much about this will be said as we go along.

2.   Then, there is the spiritually disintegrated condition of human beings, even of those who have come to notable spiritual maturation, much more those who are notably immature (even though maturing). We all have both good and bad dispositions; and, insofar as we do, we all are in varying degrees the kind of person noted in both rules 1 and 2. None of us are pure cases of spiritually maturing or regressing persons. That is why a fundamental question to consider when discerning spirits is this: What dimension of the person is being affected, what disposition?

3.   Even in the spiritually maturing dimension of a person's character, ambivalent affective responses may occur: one may, for example, experience sorrow and joy over the same event or the same truth. Thus, the repentant sinner may have sorrow over sin and joy over God's forgiving love, sadness over the harm done to others and peace because of trust in God to draw good out of our failures, or despair of progress by one's own efforts and hope in God's loving power.

4.   Spiritual consolation is in some instances prompted by the evil spirit disguised as an angel of light. We shall have to deal with this

problem at length in discussing the second set of rules, especially rules II, 3–5.

5.　Initial fear and disturbance are experienced even by spiritually mature persons when experiencing the divine in some extraordinary way.

6.　John of the Cross describes a profound spiritual desolation that can arise from the infusion of divine light. (See *Commentary*, 271–82.)

RULES I, 3–4

Preliminary Considerations (*Commentary*, 79–93, 122–24)

Before studying rules 3 and 4, we must note several things.

1.　These and all the following rules are for the person Ignatius speaks of in rule 2, one who is going from good to better, increasing in faith, hope, and charity, the one we have called a spiritually maturing person.

2.　These two rules are concerned with two experiences in the spiritual life of such a person, spiritual consolation and spiritual desolation. In his teaching on the spiritual life in general and on discernment of spirits in particular, Ignatius gives these two experiences special attention. There are several reasons for doing so. They have a strong influence on the growth or decline of faith, hope, and charity by affecting our perceptions, thoughts, and choice of actions. They also have, as we shall see, a value for discernment of spirits and discernment of God's will. Further, as we shall seen in the second set of rules for discernment of spirits, even spiritual consolations can be occasions for deceptions regarding God's will.

3.　Ignatius's intention in rules I, 3f., as analysis of these rules will show, is neither to describe consolation and desolation in the ordinary meaning of these words nor to give them a technical meaning that they do not ordinarily bear. Rather, Ignatius assumes we understand the ordinary meaning and wishes to show what he means by *spiritual* consolation or *spiritual* desolation. Therefore, before studying these rules to find out what Ignatius means by spiritual consolation and desolation, it will be wise to be as clear as we can about what constitutes any experience of consolation or desolation, whether spiritual or nonspiritual. (See the table on page 18.)

Consolation and desolation in the ordinary meaning are properly speaking affective moods, affective feelings or clusters of feelings,

STRUCTURE OF CONSOLATION AND DESOLATION

Essential Elements	Illustrations of Consolation	Illustrations of Desolation
Feelings/Mood (Consolation or Desolation properly speaking	1. Delight, joy, exultation, sweet sorrow 2. Warmth, tenderness, contentment, sense of security, cheerfulness	1. Frustration, desperation, anger, dejection 2. Loneliness, sadness, sense of worthlessness
Grounds of Feelings Extrinsic: Objects of cognitive and affective acts Intrinsic: cognitive and affective acts with these objects	Extrinsic Grounds 1. Music 2. Presence of a loved one with signs of a return of love by the loved one Intrinsic Grounds 1. Listening to the music with appreciation 2. Loving attention to loved one's presence and signs of love, with belief in that love	Extrinsic Grounds 1 Unjust situation: oppression, joblessness, being homeless, a victim of prejudice (racial, religious, sexual, class) 2. Separation from loved one by death, rejection, divorce, distance Intrinsic Grounds 1. Experience of the injustice or sensitive awareness of it in others' lives 2. 3. Experience of such separation
Consequences of feelings: thoughts, affective acts, choices, behavior	1. Humming, foot tapping, tingling in spine, remembering with tears a person or event associated with the music 2. Gratitude, desire to give to or serve the loved one, actual deeds of giving or serving	1. Rebellion, violence, social and political action to achieve justice 2. Apathy, inability to concentrate, anger tears

that is, conscious affective states as distinct from affective acts or volitions. These affective acts and affective feelings can be experienced at both the rational and the sensuous levels of affectivity. In acts we are doing something, and what we do has an object. For example, I fear what I perceive is threatening me, I desire what I perceive as valuable. In a mood or affective feeling (as we are using the word), the person is not doing anything in our ordinary meaning of doing, and the feeling has no object. For example, anxiety, emptiness, gladness, peacefulness, buoyancy, heaviness, sweetness, bitterness, and other such feelings. Three things can cause misunderstanding: (1) Sometimes the same word without any qualifying word or phrase to distinguish its meanings is used when referring to an affective feeling and to an affective act, for example, "love"; (2) as in the example just given, the act is frequently accompanied by, even experientially fused with, feeling; (3) while feelings do not have objects, they do have grounds and consequences of which the person can be clearly aware and which can be confused with objects. These grounds and consequences and their relationship to the feelings of consolation and desolation deserve fuller consideration if we are to understand what goes on in an experience of consolation or desolation and so be able to interpret Ignatius's statement about them with precision.

The grounds of the feelings of consolation are the underlying conditions or reasons or causes for the feelings. These can be cognitive or affective acts and their objects; for instance, sensations, imaginative images, intellectual insights, acts of loving, desiring, trusting, believing in being loved or in being trusted, the contemplation of beauty in nature or works of art, and so forth. These grounds can fittingly be called consolation insofar as they are the grounds of euphoric feelings, such as delight, warmth, sweetness, lightheartedness, and similar emotions. By themselves, without the feelings that they ground, the cognitive and affective acts are not consolations in any sense of the term. It is the feelings that are consolation constitutively, formally, properly speaking; the grounds are consolation only in an extended sense.

So also with desolation. It is a negative feeling or cluster of negative feelings (contrary to consolation) that constitutes desolation properly speaking; for example, feelings of loneliness, bitterness, depression, sadness, discouragement, and the like. Apart from these feelings, the acts that ground them are not desolation in any sense of the term; as the ground of desolate feelings, they can be spoken of as desolation in an extended sense.

The feelings that constitute consolation and desolation have consequences. They can influence in contrary ways the person's perception of and thinking about God, self, and other persons, things, and events. They can influence in opposite ways a person's way of deliberating for choice and action.

Each total concrete experience of consolation and desolation, then, includes some objective and/or subjective ground for affective feelings and some consequences. This total experience is consolation or desolation in the broad sense of the word. But it is the affective feeling or cluster of feelings, the mood, that constitutes consolation or desolation in the proper sense of the word and is the core component of the total experience, without which nothing else in the experience could be called a consolation or desolation in any legitimate sense of these words.

Analysis of Rules I, 3–4

The question remains, What does Ignatius see as essentially characteristic of *spiritual* consolation and *spiritual* desolation, setting them apart from any other form of consolation or desolation? To answer that question we must analyze rules 3 and 4 and then draw up a summary statement of the answer to our question. As we do so, it will become apparent that when Ignatius explains what he means by spiritual consolation and desolation, he is not at all concerned to distinguish the three factors in the essential structure of these total concrete experiences. He is content to throw out a series of illustrations that may be feelings or grounds for these feelings or even the consequences of them—trusting that taken all together these illustrations will convey a sound notion of what he means by spiritual consolation or desolation, a notion serviceable for ordinary practical purposes. Our preceding analysis of the total concrete experiences of consolation and desolation will enable us to give greater precision to what he says in this rule without in any way departing from his thought.

Analysis of Rule 3 (*Commentary*, 94–121)

In rule 3 Ignatius points out at least three, possibly four, kinds of experiences that he sees as spiritual consolation. The first description of spiritual consolation in this rule reads as follows: "I name it [spiritual] consolation when some inner motion is prompted in the person of such a kind that he begins to be aflame with love of his creator and Lord and, consequently, when he cannot love any created thing on the face of the earth in itself but only in the creator of them all." This is the paradigm form of all the spiritual consolations: all others more or less approach it. In the description there are two main elements to be noted. First, the person is said to be "aflame" with love of God and, second, cannot love any created thing except in the creator. Such love presupposes faith in God. It is, of course, an affective *act* of love, a volition; but this alone would not be a consolation properly speaking. It is a love by which the person is aflame, that is, suffused with the burning, passionate, tender *feelings* of love. These feelings are spiritual consolation properly speaking. As a consequence, the person "cannot love" any created thing except in the creator. The word "cannot" is of key significance. This statement shows how great and all-consuming the love for God is, truly an unusual experience. Such love as an act is possible without the inflamed feelings of love; it is possible in dryness and even in spiritual desolation. But then the person would not feel aflame with love and would not experience consolation.

Ignatius's second description of spiritual consolation reads: "Likewise [I call it consolation] when a person pours out tears moving to love of our Lord, whether it be for sorrow for his sins or over the passion of Christ our Lord or over other things directly ordered to his service and praise." Tears themselves are obviously not consolation but can be and, in this context, are an effect of and sign of deep feelings, which do constitute consolation—spiritual consolation when the feelings and tears spring from sorrow over sins or over the sufferings of Christ or from something else directly ordered to the service and praise of God, all of which are grounds of spiritual consolation. These feelings of sorrow also move to love of our Lord as a consequence.

The third and fourth descriptions are found in the last sentence of the rule. This sentence might be read as one description, one type of spiritual consolation; but there is reason to take it as two, the first being "every increase of hope, faith, and charity" and the second constituted by all that follows, beginning with the words "and every inward gladness."

The first of these does cause a problem. For if every growth in "hope, faith, and charity" is consolation, then consolation in Ignatius's vocabulary is an equivocal term, referring now to feelings of joy, gladness, peace, sweetness, and so on, and on other occasions referring to volitional acts without any such feelings or even with feelings directly contrary to what he usually instances as consolation. In the latter case, one who experiences bitter desolation because he feels and mistakenly thinks he is declining in love, but who in fact is perseveringly loving in deed and in truth and so continues to grow spiritually—such a one would be in consolation! One way of resolving the problem raised by Ignatius's third description of spiritual consolation is proposed in the *Commentary,* 104–7. Another solution, simpler and more likely, is to understand Ignatius as referring to "every increase of hope, faith, and charity" of which the person is aware. When a believing lover of God is aware of such growth, he will inevitably experience feelings of joy and peace. The *experienced* increase is the ground of the feelings, which constitute the consolation properly speaking.

There seems to be an order in these descriptions of spiritual consolation. They are steps in an ever widening extension of the notion of spiritual consolation from the paradigm experience, which is quite extraordinary, to the ordinary, everyday experiences indicated in the final phrases of the rule.

Analysis of Rule 4 (*Commentary,* 122–44)

The beginning of rule 4 is of great importance for understanding the whole rule and for throwing light back on rule 3. To say that everything about spiritual desolation is the contrary of what has been said about spiritual consolation means that we can extrapolate from one to the other and any knowledge we gather about one indicates something about its contrary. Therefore, the illustrations of spiritual desolation given in the rest of the rule must all be understood as feelings that are grounded in some thought and/or some affective responses in conflict with faith, hope, and charity, feelings that of themselves tend to destroy or diminish faith, hope, and charity and give rise to further thoughts and affective responses that do the same.

The Essential Features of Spiritual Consolation and Desolation (*Commentary,* 109–13, 283–90)

Basing ourselves on the Ignatian rules I, 3f., along with what he says elsewhere and using the preceding descriptive analysis of consolation and desolation in general (that is, whether nonspiritual or spiritual), we can now state concisely what constitutes the total concrete experience of *spiritual* consolation and *spiritual* desolation, what are their essential features.

Spiritual consolation as understood by Ignatius is a consolation rooted in an *experienced* increase of faith, hope, and charity, the fundamental effects of the Holy Spirit in the human mind and heart. Properly speaking, spiritual consolation is constituted by the feelings of peace in God, delight in God, spiritual warmth and sweetness, and other feelings of this nature that are the connatural consequences in affective sensibility of the experienced increase of faith, hope, and charity—unless these feelings are hindered in some way or other. As other rules make clear (see I, 7, 9, 10, 11; II, 1) and as other writings of Ignatius confirm, spiritual consolation of itself has consequences in the person consoled. Of itself it makes easier further acts of believing, hoping, and loving; gives enthusiasm for prayer and active service of God and neighbor;

inclines the one consoled toward choice and action in accord with faith, hope, and love; and therefore tends toward growth in these virtues.

Paralleling spiritual consolation, spiritual desolation is grounded in antispiritual movements in one dimension of consciousness experienced by a person who at a deeper dimension has living faith; for example, inclination to bad or relatively worthless things, temptations against faith, hope, and charity, disinterest in prayer, seeming tepidity in God's service, feeling as if separated from God, as if not loved by him, as if in discord with him. The connatural result of these antispiritual movements, cognitive and affective, in the sensibility of one who has living faith, is feelings of desolation, for example, feelings of sadness, confusion, discouragement. These desolate feelings, in turn, have consequences in the spiritually desolate person. For example, they make it harder to go on believing, hoping, and loving; they incline one to give up striving to grow spiritually ("to go from good to better"), to slack off from prayer and active service of God and neighbor. The person can resist these inclinations and prevent spiritual harm, can even grow by resistance; but of themselves, the desolate feelings tend toward effecting spiritual harm. Not every commentator on Ignatius agrees with this interpretation of what he means by spiritual consolation and desolation. For an opposing interpretation and my reasons for not accepting it, see *Commentary*, 95–97, 177f., 182–91, and especially 283–90.

RULES I, 5–14: HOW TO RESPOND
TO SPIRITUAL DESOLATION AND TEMPTATION

Of itself spiritual desolation tends toward a loss of faith, hope, and charity, to discouragement about going from good to better, and ultimately toward despair of salvation. Whether it actually has any of these results at all depends on how the person responds. That is why all the rest of the first set of rules, 5 to 14, are for helping us respond to it in a way that brings spiritual growth rather than spiritual decline. They are all concerned with spiritual desolation, therefore, and temptation. Spiritual desolation always involves temptation of one kind or another. Temptation frequently brings on spiritual desolation; even when it does not, most of Ignatius's counsels in rules I, 5–14, are relevant (*Commentary*, 147–49).

These rules easily fall into four divisions. Rules 5 and 6 are the fundamental counsels on dealing with desolation. Rules 7 to 9 are fuller developments of rule 6. Rules 10 and 11 are concerned with preparation for desolation while one is still in spiritual consolation or in spiritual calm. Rules 12 to 14 give three characteristic ways in which the evil spirit attacks us or tries to deceive us, and indicate how to uncover the deception in each case and to counterattack.

Rules I, 5–6 (*Commentary*, 147–74)

These rules give two fundamental counsels and presuppose another one that Ignatius assumes here without stating it, but one that experience teaches us needs thematic attention. We will begin with the assumed counsel for responding to spiritual desolation and then take up the two counsels that are in these rules.

1.   The unstated counsel is this: Be reflectively and explicitly aware of what is going on when you are in spiritual desolation. Name it to yourself. Recall its source and tendency (*Commentary*, 150–52). It will help here to recall what Ignatius says in *Spiritual Exercises*, [313], and to be aware of a general principle about human psychology, that reflectively attending to our own affective experiences tends to weaken their hold on us, while attending to the object of affective acts or the ground of affective feelings tends to strengthen them. Thus, attending to the objects of anger or lust tends to intensify them; reflectively attending to the affections themselves tends to weaken them.

2.   The counsel stated in rule 5 deserves great stress because it is so easy to forget it in time of desolation, with dangerous consequences. The counsel is this: During spiritual desolation stay with, hold fast to, already well made decisions; resist any inclinations to change them (*Commentary*, 152–55). The reason given in the rule for this counsel throws light on the source of spiritual consolation or desolation and shows a relationship of this rule with the last part of rule 4. A warning is in place: Beware of thinking that the Holy Spirit influences us only in consolation or that the evil spirit influences us only in desolation; the unwary reader may tend to think that Ignatius is saying just that.

3.   The counsel in rule 6 is this: Take initiative; change yourself intensely in ways contrary to desolation. What can be spoken about as the counterattack principle *(agere contra)* is a general Ignatian principle for meeting negative influences on our spiritual life. (For illustrations of his use of this principle, see *Spiritual Exercises*, [12, 13, 16, 157, 217, 319, 321, 325]). This principle underlies the counsel given in rule 6 on responding to spiritual desolation (*Commentary*, 155–62). When applied to spiritual desolation (*Commentary*, 162–74), the principle calls for such responses as increased prayer (petition), meditation, examination, and penance. An added way of counteracting desolation that is not mentioned by Ignatius is generous active service for God and neighbor. A possible reason why Ignatius omits this suggestion, so much in accord

with his spirituality, is that the rules occur in the book on making the Spiritual Exercises, and the Spiritual Exercises are not a time for active ministry (except in the nineteenth-annotation retreat).

Rules I, 7–8 (*Commentary, 175–82*)

These rules are developments of the counterattack principle given in rule 6. Rule 7 gives reasons for trusting in God and being confident of overcoming the evil spirit. (Note the possibility of misunderstanding what is said in the first sentence because of the lack of precision—as if God ever leaves us to struggle entirely on our own. It is corrected further on in the rule.) Rule 8 is a repetition of rule 6, with emphasis on the need for active and persevering resistance, with hope.

Rule I, 9: Reasons Why God Allows Spiritual Desolation (*Commentary, 182–91*)

A question arises: If spiritual desolation of itself tends to destroy faith, hope, and charity and if God loves us, why does he leave us in darkness with the anguish of feeling separated from him? This question is especially pointed in the teaching of Ignatius, who says that God loves us so much that whatever he wills for us, permissively or positively, in any concrete situation is always for our greater good, his greater glory in us. The only answer to the question coherent with Ignatius's teaching is that allowing spiritual desolation is sometimes better for us than giving us spiritual consolation and is an expression of God's merciful concern for us. To help us see how this is so, Ignatius suggests three principal ways in which desolation is sometimes better for us than consolation, ways in which desolation serves as an occasion for our faith, hope, and charity to mature or to escape harm.

Besides answering the troubling question of why God allows us to experience desolation, there is an added value in understanding the several reasons given. Being able to see what the reason is in any particular case will enable the person to respond more aptly, more effectively. Depending on which reason seems to be operative, the response will be different in each case.

A further difficulty: If spiritual desolation is allowed by God for our good, then why does Ignatius urge us to resist it, even to counterattack? Why not let it be in order to work what God wills for our good? The answer to this question is that desolation benefits us only if we strive against it; if we let it work without resistance, it will be destructive rather than beneficial. It is by struggling against it that we grow spiritually and benefit from the desolation.

Rules I, 10–11: Prepare for Desolation during Consolation (*Commentary* 192–97)

These rules are not dealing with consolation in its own right, are not a parallel with rules 5 to 9 on desolation. Rather they are a continuation of rules 5 to 9, now telling us how to prepare for and in some measure prevent desolation. The focus of attention is still on desolation and what to do about it.

Three points can be drawn out of rule 10: (1) Remember that desolation will follow consolation, (2) consider how to respond when the desolation comes, and (3) prepare for it now, renew strength to meet it. A comment on these three points. As regards the first, just as in desolation we tend to feel we shall never have consolation again and need to be told that it will come soon (rule 8), so also in consolation we tend to forget past desolation and feel that we shall never be desolate again. How, we think, can anyone ever be down and discouraged when we believe that God is so good and loving and has promised us his help, that he is with us always to bring us on to everlasting life? In both consolation and desolation, we need to hold on to the truth that our affective life is up and down, like a wave motion. If I anticipate desolation, then it is not such a shock when it comes, and I am not taken off guard and harmed before I can get hold of the situation. Regarding the second and third points, how can we go about preparing for desolation as Ignatius urges us to do? It seems that rules 5 and 6, about what to do when desolation has come, can tell us also what to do when preparing for it. We need to pray for help, putting our trust in God; we need to meditate and contemplate in order to build up our conviction of God's faithful love; we need to have a plan on how to act when desolation does come.

Rule 11 is pretty much a continuation of rule 10. It offers a twofold consideration that can help us have a true Christian attitude for meeting spiritual desolation when it does come.

Rules I, 12–14: Three Characteristic Ways in Which the Evil Spirit Attacks Us and Tries to Deceive Us and How to Deal with Each One of These (*Commentary*, 198–204)

Each rule is worthy of careful study and prayerful reflection.

In summary, but in a different order, three counsels can be drawn out of these three rules. First, seek to know yourself, your strengths and weaknesses, so as to anticipate where Satan is liable to attack and be ready to respond promptly and intelligently (rule I, 14).

Second, when attacked, make a prompt and bold counterattack, with confidence in God's presence and his power to support you (rule I, 12; see also rules I, 6, 7, 8). Third, be open with a capable spiritual counselor, one who through experience and learning understands the tactics of the evil spirit in his efforts to deceive us and the contrary tactics of the Holy Spirit in helping us (rule I, 13).

RULES II: TWO DECEPTIONS BASED ON TWO KINDS OF SPIRITUAL CONSOLATION

In rules II there are three main steps. The heading of the rules and rule 1 state the purpose and subject matter of these rules. In rules 2 and 3, Ignatius explains what he means by consolation with and consolation without previous cause and what can be the source of each. In rules 4 to 8, he describes the deception that can originate from each of the consolations and how to guard against these deceptions.

Heading and Rule 1: Purpose and Subject Matter (*Commentary,* 213–15)

The purpose of the second set of rules is the same as that of the first set. Recall the threefold purpose of the latter. The subject matter of the second set is narrowed to two surprising and subtle deceptions in which the evil spirit uses two different kinds of spiritual consolation. This subject matter requires a refinement of what has been said regarding spiritual consolation as the sign of the Holy Spirit in the first set of rules, and also of what has been said regarding the effects of the evil spirit on a person who is spiritually maturing.

Rule II, 2–3: Consolation with and without Previous Cause (*Commentary,* 216–22)

In rule II, 2, Ignatius describes consolation without previous cause and by implication consolation with previous cause. This rule is quite unclear and has led commentators to widely different interpretations of what constitutes consolation without previous cause and of how frequently it happens. In the opinion of some noted commentators, this rule is of little practical importance because the occasion for using it is so rare. In the opinion of others, consolation without previous cause is the very core of all spiritual discernment, without which any genuine discernment of spirits or of God's will is impossible. We have no time to take up these controversies here. An account of them and my way of understanding and using these two rules can be found in *Commentary*, 216–29, 243–56, and 291–313.

Only one point in rule 2 is presently important for us in order to understand rules 3 to 7, namely, the meaning of consolation with previous cause, implied by what is said about consolation without previous cause. Whatever the prompting source of consolation with previous cause (the Holy Spirit or the evil spirit; see rule 3), the influence of that source is mediated to the affectivity by some prior (at least in order of dependence, if not in the temporal order) cognitive or affective acts of the person who is consoled. In other words, there is some conscious and evident antecedent "cause" or subjective ground through which the prompting source brings about consolation properly speaking, on which the affective feelings of consolation depend.

Rule 3 indicates an ambiguity about the prompting source of the consolation with previous cause—in contrast to consolation without previous cause, which God alone can effect. Either a good or an evil spirit, with contrary purposes, can prompt consolation with previous cause.

Rules II, 4–7: Deception Based on Consolation with Previous Cause (*Commentary, 222–42*)

Rule II, 4, describes the deception that can be worked by an evil spirit beginning from this kind of consolation (*Commentary*, 222–27). The starting point of the deception is said to be "good and holy thoughts." Note in rules II, 4f., the focus on *thoughts* which ground or follow on spiritual consolation, the initial thoughts and the progression of thoughts. Through the progression or process of thoughts (by association or by speciously logical reasoning), the initial thoughts lead to various antispiritual consequences. Various kinds will be noted in rule 5. Ignatius does not say so, but it seems sure and is important to note that there has to be a continuity (not necessarily temporal) in the process, each step after the first having some dependence on the previous one (see *Commentary*, 225f.).

A question about consolation in rules II, 3f., concerns spiritual and nonspiritual consolation. Is Ignatius thinking of a truly spiritual consolation or of one that is only seemingly so? There is no need to delay over this question here. For an answer, see *Commentary*, 229f.

Rule II, 5, tells us how to uncover the deception and the evil spirit at its source (*Commentary*, 227–35). The principle of discernment involved in uncovering the deception is this: Whatever comes from the Holy Spirit is good through and through. Consequently, unless the beginning, the middle, and the end of the total concrete experience are all good, the whole experience is to be judged as prompted by the evil spirit. (But remember what was said above about the necessity of continuity in the experience.) Therefore, Ignatius counsels us to be watchful of what follows on the good beginning of the total experience, alert for any sign of the evil spirit. If he is at work, this sign will surely appear. Some signs to look for are untrue thoughts, unreasonable thoughts, thoughts opposed to faith, hope, and charity; affections that are sinful or constitute spiritual desolation; thoughts and/or affections that distract from good works; inclinations toward and/or plans for a lesser good than one had previously intended.

Rule II, 6, tells us what to do immediately when deception is uncovered (*Commentary,* 235–42).

Rule II, 7, shows why we can be confident of uncovering the deception from consolation with previous cause (*Commentary,* 237–41).

It is important that we keep a balanced attitude toward possible deception of this sort. There is no need to be worrisome or suspicious of every spiritual consolation or to analyze it reflectively, thereby suppressing it. Rather we should be calm and trusting in the Holy Spirit, allowing the experience to develop, assuming that it is from the Holy Spirit until shown otherwise, but remaining alert to any sign of the evil spirit if it should show up. If he is acting, the sign of this will certainly appear (*Commentary,* 231f.).

Rule II, 8: Deception Based on Consolation without Previous Cause (*Commentary,* 243–56)

Ignatius thinks that neither consolation without previous cause nor deceptive thoughts and attractions integral with it can be prompted by the evil spirit. Both the consolation and the thoughts or attractions are from God. The main point of rule II, 8, is the necessity of discerning the precise time of the actual consolation without previous cause as distinct from the following time of afterglow. For during that afterglow plans or reasoning can occur to us that we think are integral with the actual consolation and therefore certainly from God. The truth is that such thoughts need prolonged and careful critical examination (*Commentary,* 243–46).

It might be suggested that what Ignatius says in rule II, 8, can profitably and without conflict with his thought be extended to consolation with previous cause. If so, then we can have a principle that applies to all experiences of consolation accompanied by attractions to or plans for ways of acting: *Never* act on these without first subjecting the experiences to critical examination (*Commentary*, 251–56; *DGW*, 142–53).

A Series of Questions for Critical Examination of Interior Motions

It might be practically helpful to draw up a brief series of questions (based on *Commentary* and "Explanatory Notes") to be answered in any discernment of spirits.

1. Is the person having the experience predominantly a spiritually maturing person, striving to go from good to better, or a spiritually regressing person, going from bad to worse?

2. What dimension of the person, what disposition, is being affected?

3. If the experience involves consolation, is it a spiritual consolation? (*DGW*, 143). Questions for discerning whether it is spiritual: Is the consolation rooted in living faith, so that the person would not experience consolation if he or she were without such faith? Are the thoughts that ground the consolation or are consequences of it in accord with the Gospel and with sound reason?

4. If the consolation is spiritual, is it prompted by the Holy Spirit or by an evil spirit? (*DGW*, 143). Is the total experience good not only at the beginning but also at the middle and end?

5. If the experience involves a desolation, is it spiritual? Some signs that a desolation is spiritual: It derives from antispiritual thoughts or affective acts; of itself, it tends to weaken faith, hope, and charity.

FOUR

A METHOD FOR STUDYING CASES

M any years of teaching graduate theology students courses on Ignatian discernment and giving workshops have convinced me that serious case study is necessary for coming to a sound and ready understanding of Ignatian teaching and, above all, for developing skill in the practice of it. The method proposed here for studying cases demands much time and exacting mental effort. Lazy and superficial case study is not merely useless but can easily lead to a dangerous illusion of competence and the risk of spiritual malpractice on oneself or others. If one is unable or unwilling to dedicate the time and energy required for a thorough and careful study, it would be better not to undertake the study of discernment at all. It would be much wiser and safer to rely on some guide known to be learned and experienced in helping people to discern spirits and to discern God's will. Under the guidance of such a person, one can, in the course of time, assimilate some unorganized practical counsels that can be employed on one's own for spiritual discernment in less difficult situations, while avoiding the grave danger in more difficult situations that results from judgments rooted in superficial knowledge or in plainly erroneous ways of thinking that are fallaciously presumed to be the fruit of serious study.

This recommended method for studying cases has seven steps to be taken successively, none after the first to be attempted until the previous step has been completed.

1. The first step is a necessary preparation for any study of the cases. This step is a serious study of "Explanatory Notes on Ignatius' Rules of Discernment of Spirits" (or, preferably, of the book on which these notes are based, *A Commentary on St. Ignatius' Rules for Discernment of Spirits*). The questions for reflection accompanying each case are intended to call attention to some elements of Ignatius's teaching as it is interpreted in those notes, and the proposed responses to these questions are in accord with that interpretation. Consequently, these responses cannot be readily understood or evaluated without a good grasp of what is in "Explanatory Notes."

After the study of these notes, steps 2 to 6 can be carried out for each case in turn.

2. The second step is to read attentively the statement of the case history for the case to be studied.

3. The third step is to think out and write down your response to each question for reflection posed after the statement of the particular case now being studied. Do this as well as you can on the basis of your preceding study of "Explanatory Notes" in step 1. If there is any question you cannot answer now, leave it for step 4.

The questions placed after the statement of the case do not necessarily cover every important aspect of the case; but, one hopes, they will serve the purpose of stimulating hard thinking, careful analysis, and precise application of principles. If those studying the case want to add further questions, that will be all to the good.

While discernment of spirits is essential to spiritual direction, it does not encompass all that is essential to it. The questions for reflection given with each case and the proposed responses to these questions are not intended to deal with all that a spiritual director might want to take up with the person whose experience is recounted in the case. The focus of study in this book is limited to discernment of spirits. If the person or group studying a case wishes to go beyond that limit, there is no reason not to do so—and to do so profitably. Only be mindful that if doing so withdraws attention from the focus of this study, to the extent that it does so it will for now be a distraction from learning how to do discernment of spirits.

4. After completing your responses to the questions about this case, the next step, the fourth, will be to study again those pages referred to in the **Reading** that follows the questions. The pages referred to in *Commentary* and "Explanatory Notes" do not necessarily touch on everything in these documents that can be relevant to the case being studied. They will serve, one may hope, to give some leads to the main teachings of Ignatius applicable to the case at hand. After studying the pages referred to, see whether what you learn from them calls for a revision of anything in the responses you gave in step 3 or enables you to answer any question you left unanswered in that step. Are there matters in the reading that you do not understand or with which you disagree? If so, note them for inquiry and discussion.

5. The fifth step is to go through the proposed responses offered in chapter 6 to each of the questions for reflection on the particular case being studied. Does your response given in step 3 and, perhaps, corrected in step 4 agree with the one proposed here? If not, which response do you consider more in accord with Ignatius's thought? Be

assiduous in trying to understand the response given in the book, and be open-minded in evaluating it. On the one hand, demand convincing reasons for thinking that the response given in the book is more accurate than yours. On the other hand, demand of yourself convincing reasons for holding to your own opinion. If you are uncertain about which response is correct, leave it as a question for now, to be pondered and, as opportunity offers, to be discussed later on with others who you judge have a good understanding of Ignatian teaching.

6. The sixth step is what might be called playing with the case. This playing with a case can serve to sharpen one's knowledge of principles and one's skill in applying them, developing sensitivity to circumstances and flexibility of judgment. All the cases are more or less incomplete and their character subject to change by data added or subtracted. Sometimes the case as given is complete enough to call for a certain response to a question asked about it, but would call for a different response if some factor was added or subtracted. At other times, the case as given is not complete enough to allow for any response save that of uncertainty. Patience to wait for accurate and adequate information is essential for spiritual discernment; jumping to judgments without sufficient or accurate information is to court error and possible harm. The capacity to recognize when it is necessary to wait and inquire, the capacity to sway with the changing case as information is added or misunderstanding is cleared up, all this can be developed by playing with cases in a learning situation, adding now one factor, now another, deleting now one factor, now another, and seeing how this affects what principles are relevant and how they are to be applied.

7. The seventh step is to carry on your study with some other person (or, preferably, persons) who has also completed steps 1 to 6 or whom you know to be already expert in discernment. Each of you can present to the other for criticism or confirmation the results you have arrived at from steps 1 to 5 and, if they differ, work toward agreement. Working together, several can play with the cases more effectively than any single person can and also do role playing. This kind of collaboration can be immensely profitable for learning.

FIVE

CASES WITH QUESTIONS FOR REFLECTION

●   *Case 1*   ●

Carlo goes to the college chapel for noon Mass. The reading for the day is from Gal. 5:16–24. The homilist focuses on verse 22: "But the fruit of the Spirit is love, joy, peace, patience, kindness, goodness, faithfulness." Peace and joy, he says, are *the* signs of the Holy Spirit. He quotes also from noted spiritual writers who emphasize this point and relates it especially to the teaching of St. Ignatius of Loyola on discernment of spirits.

Carlo has for some time now felt very dry when he prays. He is saddened because God seems absent from his life. What the homilist said convinces him that the Holy Spirit cannot be present and active in his life, that he must have turned away from God. He feels discouraged about ever becoming a really good Christian.

In this state of mind, he comes to one of his teachers in whose learning and experience and good judgment he has great trust. He opens up to her and asks for help.

➤   *Questions for Reflection (in step 3 of "A Method for Studying Cases")*

1. Is Carlo a spiritually maturing or spiritually regressing person? Explain.
2. Does rule I, 1, or I, 2, apply to Carlo? Why?
3. Is he experiencing spiritual, antispiritual, or nonspiritual movements? Explain and justify your answer.
4. By what spirit is Carlo being moved?
5. What does Carlo need to have explained to him in the Ignatian rules for discernment of spirits in order to help him understand the experience that he has come to talk about?

Reading (in step 4 of "Method"): *Commentary,* 56–78, 90–93, 109f., 127–40; "Explanatory Notes," 15–17, 19–22[1]

● *Case 2* ●

[This case is found in Mark 10:17–22.]

And as Jesus was setting out on his journey, a man ran up and knelt before him and asked him, "Good Teacher, what must I do to inherit eternal life?" And Jesus said to him, "Why do you call me good? No one is good but God alone. You know the commandments: 'Do not kill, do not commit adultery, do not steal, do not bear false witness, do not defraud, honor your father and mother.'" And he said to him, "Teacher, all these I have observed from my youth." And Jesus, looking upon him, loved him and said to him, "You lack one thing; go, sell what you have and give to the poor and you will have treasure in heaven; and come, follow Me." At that saying his countenance fell and he went away sorrowful; for he had great possessions.

And Jesus looked around and said to his disciples, "How hard it will be for those who have riches to enter the kingdom of God!"

➤ *Questions for Reflection (in step 3 of "Method")*

1. Is there any evidence in this passage to indicate what kind of person the young man is, spiritually regressing or spiritually maturing?

2. What spirit, good or evil, is affecting him? What are your reasons for your answer to this question?

3. We can assume that when Jesus calls the young man to follow him, the Holy Spirit moves him within toward doing so. Now, according to rules I, 2, and II, 7, we should expect that when the Holy Spirit acts on a spiritually maturing person, the person will experience spiritual consolation; but what the young man in fact experiences is sadness. Is Ignatius's teaching in conflict with this incident in the Gospel?

Reading (in step 4 of "Method"): *Commentary,* 72–77, 238f; "EN," 16f., 19–22

● *Case 3* ●

[This is really a series of obviously incompletely stated cases with a limited purpose of calling attention to the distinction between spiritual,

---

[1] Hereafter "Explanatory Notes" will be cited as "EN."

antispiritual, and nonspiritual inner movements and showing how often what is known about someone's experience of consolation or desolation is inadequate for making a sound judgment about it.]

1. I find out that someone I admire and love very much responds to me in the same way. I feel elated, full of joy.

2. Later I discover that I was mistaken; the person I so admire and love really has no use for me. I feel hurt and sad at this discovery.

3. This experience (in para. 2 above) disturbs my prayer and distracts me from the needs of others.

4. Because of this experience, I feel mistreated by God and am tempted to think I am unloved by him.

5. I attend a liturgy during which I am delighted by the beautiful singing and eloquent preaching and the real warmth among the people who are there.

6. I think of my sins and of Christ's sufferings. I am saddened, I weep, I feel depressed. I think, What's the use of trying? I am no good.

7. I pass an exam brilliantly. I feel happy about it. I thank God.

8. I appear to be very successful in my spiritual ministry: many people thank me and praise my work. As a consequence, I experience joy.

9. Because of my success and the praise that I receive, I am grateful to God.

➤ *Question for Reflection (in step 3 of "Method")*

Assuming that the person in each of these cases is a spiritually maturing person (as in rule 2), do you, in each of them, without any further information, find evidence for judging that the experience related is a spiritual consolation or desolation or nonspiritual consolation or desolation; or do you think that the information provided is insufficient for any such judgment?

Reading (in step 4 of "Method"): *Commentary,* 109–21, 127–38, 141–43; "EN," 17–19, 21f.

● *Case 4* ●

[Among the first and one of the most intense and influential persons in the antislavery movement in the United States was the eminent Quaker John Woolman. In the three paragraphs given below, we see how the heart of this predominantly good Christian was affected by good and evil spirits while he was growing toward the courage of his convictions. These paragraphs, except for what is in brackets, are quotations from Woolman's diary as presented in Piet Penning de Vries, S.J., "Quaker

Experience and Ignatian Principles," *Spiritual Life* (Summer 1972): 128, 130, 132.]

1. Within a year after my coming to Mount Holly, my master having a negro sold her and told me to write a bill of sale. The thought of writing an instrument of slavery for one of my fellow creatures gave me trouble, and I was distressed in my mind about it. At length I considered that I was hired by the year, it was my master bid me do it, and that it was an elderly man, a member of our Society, who bought her, so I wrote the bill of sale. But on the executing of it I was depressed in my mind and said before my master and the friend that I believed slavekeeping to be a practice inconsistent with the Christian religion; saying so abated my uneasiness; yet as often as I reflected seriously upon it I thought I should have been clearer if, leaving all consequences, I had craved to be excused from it, as a thing against my conscience; for such it was.

[Later, Woolman was sent by Quaker leadership to minister to Quaker slave holders. Again he experienced inner turmoil. To avoid any appearance whatsoever of compromise or collaboration, Woolman refused to accept hospitality or any kind of gift from people who kept slaves. How he dreaded the possibility of thus offending the members of his own religious Society.]

2. The prospect of so weighty a work, and of being so distinguished from many whom I esteem before myself, brought me very low, and such were the conflicts of my soul that I had a near sympathy with the prophet in the time of his weakness, when he said: "If thou deal thus with me, kill me, I pray thee, out of hand, if I have found favour in the sight." Then I soon saw that this proceeded from the want of a full resignation to Him. Many were the afflictions which attended me, and in great abasement, with many tears, my cries were to the Almighty for His gracious and fatherly assistance, and then after a time of deep trial, I was favoured to understand the state mentioned by the Psalmist more clearly than ever I had before, to wit: "My soul is even as a weaned child." Being thus helped to sink down into resignation, I felt a deliverance from the tempest in which I had been sorely exercised, and in calmness of mind went forward, trusting that the Lord, as I faithfully attended to Him, would be a counsellor to me in all difficulties.

3. [On July 9, 1757, Woolman wrote in his diary:]

As I was riding along in the morning my mind was deeply affected in a sense I had of the want of Divine aid to support me in the various difficulties which attended me, and in an uncommon distress of mind I cried in secret to the Most High, "Oh Lord be merciful, I beseech Thee, to Thy poor afflicted creature!" After some time I felt inward relief. [Later he wrote:] From the time of my entering Maryland I have been much under sorrow, which of late so increased upon me that my mind was almost overwhelmed, and I may say with the Psalmist, "In my distress I called upon the Lord, and cried to my God," who in infinite goodness, looked upon my affliction, and in my private retirement sent the Comforter for my relief, for which I humbly bless His Holy name.

➤ *Question for Reflection (in step 3 of "Method")*

      In each of the above paragraphs, what spiritual or antispiritual movements do you discern that Woolman is experiencing? What Ignatian rule or rules can you cite in support of your answer?

Reading (in step 4 of "Method"): *Commentary,* 30–34, 56–70, 72–78, 175–91, 198–204; "EN," 11–26

●　*Case 5*　●

[What follows is, with some editing, from a letter received by a retreat director, who, with the correspondent's permission, sent the letter to me to be used as a case if I so wished. It was written a month after the retreat mentioned by the writer and concerns an experience that began on the way home from the retreat house after a retreat filled with spiritual consolation.]

Dear Marge,

1. I have been thinking about you and I had planned to write sooner, but this is the first chance I've had. I wanted you to know how important my "miniretreats" have been, what an impact they seem to be having on my life. I think it is even more apparent to me now after being home for some weeks than it was while I was actually there at the retreat house.

2. That experience I had as I was leaving after my retreat a month ago made quite an impression on me. It certainly took me by surprise! My mind was in such confusion that I couldn't comprehend what was happening to me. I didn't understand how I could feel so bad so fast, after feeling so good for so long. On my way home I was second-guessing my entire retreat and felt that due to my failure it had been a complete waste of time. I figured that I must have some serious problem and that maybe I had been dishonest by not bringing it up during the retreat. And since I didn't even know what the "problem" was, I concluded that I was probably incapable of making a "good" retreat because I was incapable of being honest and open. The thought came to me that I should not waste your time and mine with these retreats.

3.   When I thought of calling you about it, I ran into still more obstacles. I felt that I really had no right to bother you—after all, my retreat was over. If things weren't resolved during the retreat, that was my own fault. And then there was *fear*. I felt very vulnerable because I was going to be revealing something to you and I didn't know what it was. I didn't know if it was emotional, psychological, spiritual, sinful— and it was so uncharacteristic of anything that had come up at any of our meetings. I was afraid of what you would think of me, and I was afraid of what you might say to me.

4.   So it was truly the grace of God that prompted me to make that phone call, and your words and prayers revealed the truth to me. I realize now more than ever how much God loves me, how much I need him; and I am more determined than ever to "keep my eyes fixed on Jesus," to follow him, to serve him, to do his will. There is nothing that he could ask of me that would be more painful than the pain of being separated from him.

5.   I am really thankful that I was able to talk to you about it. Looking back now, it all seems so clear that it could not possibly have been God's voice telling me these things, but there was just enough truth in it to make me unsure. After all, it *is* difficult for me to open up and share. (I think I even shared that with you during the retreat.) But God is so patient!

6.   I realize also the value of my weekend retreats. Since I was being tempted to abandon them, I realize I need to continue to make them a priority in my life, and I hope you will continue to be my spiritual director.

7.   The important thing to me about this entire experience is that God was with me even though I was unaware of his presence, and he brought me through it. I know he will be with me through all the challenges I face.

8.   There is so much more I could say about what God has been doing in my life, but I will be up all night. He is compassionate. He is faithful.

With love and gratitude,

Lucia

➤ *Questions for Reflection (in step 3 of "Method")*

1.   What Ignatian rules for discernment of spirits help to understand the experience described in paragraph 2 of Lucia's letter? Explain your answer.

2. What Ignatian rules would clearly apply to the experience described in paragraphs 3 to 5?

3. What rule is illustrated in paragraph 6?

4. What rule is illustrated in paragraphs 7 and 8?

Reading (in step 4 of "Method"): *Commentary,* 57–70, 200–204; "EN," 11–26

● *Case 6* ●

[This experience is told in the first person by the one who had it.]

1. For several months we had lived in our new home some miles from the city when my decision to go on a week-long retreat came up. Matt, my husband, agreed to be home with the family. It was holiday time, and there would be older children home as well. The day I was to leave, two friends from our former parish in the city came out unexpectedly. I prepared dinner, we all had a good family time, and were having fun; and then it was time for one of the children to drive me into the city so that I would be there at the specified time.

2. I met the Sister who was to direct this retreat. I was the only person on retreat in that huge building—just me and the whistling radiator. I met with my director once a day; she gave me points for meditation and we talked about the prayer afterwards. It went pretty well until the fourth day.

3. At that point the thought came that I belonged at home; I was selfish to be away from my family; prayer is better within the home and at work rather than on my knees in an empty room with a hot, whistling radiator. This thought unsettled me. None of the meditations went well. I could not find light in Holy Scripture. I was restless and roamed the room like a caged bear. I went through my notes, the papers I had brought, flipped through the Bible, cleared out my purse. In it were two thin dimes. Placing them on the dresser, I looked at them, remembered the pay phone near the main entrance, and began to think about home. I said nothing to the Sister whom, I decided, I did not like and who, I now thought, most certainly did not know beans from bones about prayer, life, or people in general. The time passed slowly, the dimes became more tantalizing; and during one prayer session, I picked them up and decided to call home when the hour was completed.

4. This I did. I was calling to ask my husband to come and bring me home. He was stunned to hear my voice. I told him what I thought and suggested that I come home. He said very firmly, "Stella, you are there for the family, not for yourself. Go back to your prayer, and I will pick you up in four days."

5. I was crushed. We both hung up. I returned to my room, knelt by the bed and wept. My hands went to the Bible on the bed and I opened it with no purpose whatsoever. It was opened to Eph. 6:10–16. I read it. Lights came on in my head, and I realized, slow learner that I am, that what had been going on was a siege, with the bad spirit manipulating me in my weak areas.

6. When my next conference time arrived, I laid everything on the table to the Sister, everything from my personal feelings to the phone call, to the Scripture. From that point on, the entire retreat changed. Prayer became alive and fruitful, I was peaceful. A gift was given to me in four words from John's prologue, "Love following upon love." A gift was given for our family, a way of prayer which Sister gave to me, the *collatio,* or little meal, as a way of prayer. It caught on with the whole family. In addition, chapter 6 of Ephesians became a prayer for Matt and me. We use it every day.

➤ *Questions for Reflection (in step 3 of "Method")*

1. Which Ignatian rules throw light on the events in paragraph 3?
2. Which Ignatian rules throw light on the events in paragraphs 4 and 5?
3. Which Ignatian rules throw light on the events in paragraph 6?

Reading (in step 4 of "Method"): *Commentary,* 56–70, 150–74, 198–204; "EN," 11–24, 26–28

●   *Case 7*   ●

[The author of this case informed me that, although his name is not Kevin and the circumstances of his life are not the same as Kevin's, nevertheless, "I am Kevin and this was my life some years ago." With a few changes to preserve anonymity, this story is just as he wrote it.]

1. Kevin is thirty-seven years old, married to a woman who lacks emotional warmth and cannot bear children. A prayerful man, for ten years he has taught theology at a university. An excellent teacher with a sound background in spirituality, he is much sought after as a counselor and speaker and usually accedes to the many requests for his services. Although he has scholarly ability and ambition to write, his busy schedule prevents him from doing so.

2. During the past few months, Kevin has felt very tired, lonely, frustrated, and somewhat confused about his life. His prayer life has diminished.

3. He used to have a spiritual director who was a great help to him, but lately he finds himself too busy to make the hour's drive to see

her. Besides, he thinks that she is just as busy as he is and doesn't really have the kind of time he would need to talk about what is going on in him. Anyway, he has lost confidence in her approach and doesn't feel that it really is what he needs. Maybe it's time to be his own director. After all, he does direct other people.

4. There is one real joy in his life now, his relationship with Jessica. With her he feels at ease and free. They talk about everything. Sometimes they express their love physically. Kevin has told himself that this experience is a gift of God—or, at least, nothing harmful.

5. But now he wonders about it: if it is a good experience, why does he feel so guilty? He figures that he should put an end to the physical expression, talk this over with Jessica, and go to confession. But there is really nobody around whom he would consider a good confessor for him. All the priests at the downtown church are quite old, and he doesn't want to go to the local pastor because he knows him too well. Kevin thinks that it doesn't make that much difference at this point. Confession can wait; after all, his "fundamental option" is still for God.

6. Kevin makes another try at remaining faithful to his work and marriage and taking some time for prayer every once in a while. His prayer is usually dry and distracted. As time goes on, he begins to feel angry at God. He feels that God has left him alone, that he is asking him to do all this work and is not there to support him when he needs help. The only relationship he wants (the one with Jessica) he can't have. He feels as if he just wants to give up trying to lead a good Christian life, give up trying to be a spiritual leader, give up trying to make something of his marriage, continue his relationship with Jessica, and just live like so many others he knows. Like them, he's only human.

7. He decides not to make a quick decision. Any decision will affect a good many people and perhaps the rest of his life. So he decides that during vacation he will go up to a little cottage in the mountains for two weeks where he can be alone and make a retreat in solitude.

8. During his first day up there, Kevin prays some psalms and reads some favorite scriptural passages. He is very restless and nothing is happening with the Lord. He gets discouraged, figures this is a waste of time, and is tempted to end the retreat right now.

9. The second afternoon he goes swimming in a mountain stream. As he lies naked on a rock to dry off, he feels a great sense of God's presence, who loves him as his own dear creation. "Naked I came forth from my mother's womb and naked shall I return" keeps coming up from within him. He feels the Lord's love as his own personal salvation

history is revealed to him; he feels special to God. He is elated and gives praise and thanks to God. His feeling lasts for a couple of days.

10. One morning some days later, Kevin goes down to a mountain stream and finds a couple there kissing and caressing each other. The woman takes their baby and begins to nurse her at the breast. Kevin is overcome with a deep sense of loss that this is not part of his life and begins to weep. He walks along a path and is confused and feels as if there were darkness all around him. He is angry at God again. He feels cheated, lured by God and then left alone.

11. As he continues to walk, his anger and confusion subside. The thought comes that what has just happened is the Lord's way of telling him that he should leave his wife and marry Jessica. Why else would God let him feel so lonely and give him such desires? At this thought, Kevin feels alive and happy. He decides to go home the next morning and make plans with Jessica.

12. That night he cannot sleep. He is restless; he gets up and goes outside. The moon is shining so he goes to the stream, takes off his clothes and wades. From his depths he hears the question, "Can you follow me naked, poor, dispossessed of all things? Follow me, I will never leave you. Let me be your all." Kevin knows it is the Lord; he feels a deep peace and desires to follow Christ dispossessed. He spends the next days in deep prayer, with growing confidence and peace. He returns home with renewed courage to face his life as it is, trusting God to see him through and give it a meaning.

➤   *Study of This Case*

Instead of following the usual steps 3, 4, and 5, read the reflections given by the author of the case as they are presented below in the section "Proposed Responses to Questions for Reflections." Go through it paragraph by paragraph, and see whether you agree with the author's own understanding of his experience. If not, why not? How would you understand it?

●   *Case 8*   ●

[This experience is related by the one who went through it while studying Ignatian spirituality and making the Spiritual Exercises according to the nineteenth annotation. It is an ordinary low-key experience, a good illustration of several Ignatian rules.]

1. During the first part of the prayer, I could not settle down to pray. I was sitting in my room, but the thought kept going through my mind that maybe I should be in the chapel. I felt restless, while my

mind was having a debate about where I would most find the Lord's presence. I finally decided to stay in my room, but I was still feeling restless. I next started wondering how I would pray. I did not resonate with Ignatius's meditation at this point in the Exercises. I would, I felt sure, do better with a different way of meditation, yet I wanted to learn Ignatius's way. So my thoughts went on. The inner debate just aggravated my feelings of restlessness. Throughout, I was asking the Lord where and how he wanted me to pray, but my restlessness and inner debate were leading to confusion.

2.   Suddenly I recognized what was going on (because of our class on discernment) and prayed against it. Suddenly the inner debate stopped and I felt strongly attracted to a particular Scripture passage. The prayer time went well: I was peaceful and able to allow the Lord to reveal the meaning of the Scripture passage and its application to my life. The challenge of the Scripture to my sinfulness was peaceful, with a strong sense of the Lord's loving acceptance and transforming power.

➤ *Questions for Reflection (in step 3 of Method")*

Which Ignatian rules help to discern what spirits are acting on this person in the experience described

1.   in paragraph 1? Explain.
2.   in paragraph 2? Explain.

Reading (in step 4 of "Method"): *Commentary,* 54–63; "EN," 15f.

● *Case 9* ●

[The following passage is taken from St. Augustine's *Confessions,* bk. 8, chap. 7. The time of the event recounted here is many years after Augustine had begun his search for wisdom and shortly before his conversion. He had by this time studied many philosophical and religious ways of thought and found that none of them other than the Christian faith made sense to him. The passage describes Augustine's inner experience on hearing the account by Ponticianus about the conversion to Christ of two of his young friends.]

Thus, while Ponticianus was relating these events, I felt a gnawing within me and a terrible confusion from horrifying shame. When he had finished his story and accomplished what he had come for, he departed and I turned to myself. What did I not say within my soul to make it follow me as I strove to go after you [God]? Yet it [my soul] drew back; without excuse, it refused to follow. All arguments were already used and refuted. Only mute trembling remained. It dreaded as it would death to be restrained from its customary indulgence, by which it was wasting away to death.

➤ *Questions for Reflection (in step 3 of "Method")*

1. Which Ignatian rule, I, 1 or 2, applies to Augustine's experience described in this passage? Explain.

2. Do any other rules cast light on this experience? How?

Reading (in step 4 of "Method"): *Commentary,* 47–69, 175–78, 198–204; "EN," 14–16, 25f.

● *Case 10* ●

[This case is fictional, devised for teaching. Joanna has a poor self-image. She is usually uneasy with strangers. She is disturbed by new ways of thinking and acting and tends to react with fear and harshness to those who speak and act in accord with these new ways. She is, however, a kind person who does love Christ, who wants very much to be accepted with love by others, and who is sensitive to beauty, sympathetic with anyone who suffers, and capable of friendship even with one or another individual whose views clash with hers. One of these friends, Lucy, pressures Joanna to come with her to a charismatic meeting. She reluctantly consents. What follows is a description of what went on in Joanna before, during, and after attending the meeting.]

1. On the way to the meeting, Joanna feels anxious and gloomy, a bit resentful toward Lucy for getting her into this.

2. On arriving, she finds the people she meets to be generally balanced and intelligent and, to her surprise, finds herself welcomed with genuinely warm affection. All seem glad to have her there. A sense of relief and deep satisfaction replaces the fear and resentment; she feels a glow of affection toward these people.

3. As the meeting progresses, Joanna is delighted with the beauty of their singing to God in tongues.

4. As she begins to feel more and more at ease, she is able to remember that these good people, their warmth toward her, the beauty of song, her own capacity to appreciate and enjoy these, are all God's gifts and she gives thanks and praise to God for his gifts.

5. Then she remembers the meaning of gift: It expresses love. She is filled with peace and joy in the belief that God loves her and is telling her so in these gifts.

6. During the meeting a man gives a testimony of God's mercy in his life, relating the misery of his life before he was converted to God.

As she listens, Joanna's sympathetic heart is touched. She thinks of some persons she knows whose lives are empty of meaning and joy, full of bitterness and despair. A great sadness comes over her and a temptation to doubt God's love and providential care for these people. She prays for her own greater trust in God and for the healing of these people.

7. By the time she leaves the meeting, her heart is at peace and even touched with a quiet joy because of the trust she has that God loves the people she prayed for even as he loves her, and so he will take care of them.

8. When she gets home and reflects on the whole experience, she remembers how often she has put up barriers between herself and others who, like the people at the meeting, really do love God and want to be accepted by her in Christian love. She remembers how harshly and unjustly she judged the charismatics and spoke of them with scorn. She feels ashamed of herself, very sad, despairing of her own power to do better. She weeps.

9. The following morning, for some reason inexplicable to her, Joanna experiences very negative emotions about the night before. She has a lurking suspicion she has been taken in, trapped into foolish sentimentality. She is again angry with Lucy and tempted to think the charismatics are, after all, sort of kooky.

10. Later that day her feelings turn around. She feels bad for having resented Lucy, who is only trying to be helpful, and for thinking harshly of the charismatics who were obviously so good to her and so sincere in praising God. She sees herself as ugly and unlovable. She begins to be confused and discouraged about trying to grow as a Christian. It's too hard to know what God really wants of us, she thinks; we are too weak and easily confused. Does God even care anyway?

11. Strangely enough, the next day and for some days thereafter Joanna becomes very tranquil. She has a peaceful sense of God's loving presence, a drawing to prayer of praise and thanks, a more gentle attitude toward those who before aroused her defenses by their different views on Christian life.

➤   *Question for Reflection (in step 3 of "Method")*

For each numbered step of Joanna's experience, can you from the data given make a sound conjecture that she is experiencing non-spiritual consolation, spiritual consolation, nonspiritual desolation, or spiritual desolation? Explain briefly.

Reading (in step 4 of "Method"): *Commentary,* 47–63, 103–21; "EN," 14–22

• *Case 11* •

[The following three anecdotes are told by Hugh T. Kerr in "Discerning the Presence," *Theology Today* 44, no. 3 (October 1988): 305f., 308. Only the paragraph numbers are inserted for easy reference.]

1. Consider the following three personal episodes. As I was delivering mail in the health-care clinic attached to the retirement community where I now live, a black woman "companion," as we call the uniformed attendants who care for wheelchair patients, was playing "Amazing Grace" on the piano in the social room. I guessed she was not a "paper" musician, for her notes, rhythm, and variations were very much her own. It was a sort of "stride" style, but slow and deliberate; and every now and then she punctuated the familiar words with her own refrain—"Praise God!" Her patient was slumped over in her wheelchair as nurses, doctors, volunteers, and maintenance people passed by detached and unobserving. I stood for a few minutes quietly at the side, caught the eye of the piano player and muttered a somewhat embarrassed "Thank you." Then I left.

2. The annual Princeton Theological Seminary commencement is held in the neo-Gothic chapel of Princeton University. The sacred space, which so often during the academic year is sparsely occupied by university students and faculty, is always jammed to the full for the seminary commencement. As I was making my way toward the chapel through a crowded town square, I found myself behind a family comprising a father, a mother, an older daughter, and a younger, severely handicapped, daughter. They were dressed in their best and were heading toward the chapel, perhaps to see another member of the family graduate. As I was walking behind them, the spastic daughter suddenly tripped over a cobblestone and fell flat on her face. I was about to intervene; but the family, who had apparently dealt with this kind of situation before, without a word quickly picked up the stricken person, who, curiously, had a benign smile on her face. Later, in the narthex of the chapel, I saw the family happily making their way toward the few empty spaces in the back pews. I felt somewhat foolish as I whispered audibly, "Jesus, be with that person." And later, I reflected that Jesus, too, had faltered, perhaps stumbling over the rough roadway, and that he needed someone to help. I never saw any of them again.

3. In the television documentary series known as *Our World*, the time span for a recent broadcast covered "Liberation Summer 1944." Toward the end of the program, Linda Ellerbee, one of the narrators, told about her father, an army sergeant who always hoped to see Paris but who died before the liberation. Thirty-four years later, she made her own trip to Paris and raised a toast: "Here's to Paris, France. To the

Americans who saw her in 1944 and to the one who never saw her at all." And then she added: "Liberation Summer and my daddy are gone forever. The salute still stands." Haven't we read some place, "Honor your father and . . ."?

4. It may seem preposterous to suggest that all three episodes, within a few days of each other, became fixed in memory as extraordinary experiences, bordering on immediate and certain awareness of something numinous and sacred. Are such personal episodes, which every one has at one time or another, authentic theophanies or merely intense, subjective, emotional reactions? [After reflecting on accounts in the Bible and in contemporary reports of God's apparent intervention in people's lives, Kerr asks a question:] What about the three personal experiences with which we began? I really haven't any idea how to evaluate whether they were authentic theophanies or merely subjective fantasies.

➤ *Questions for Reflection (in step 3 of "Method")*

1. In paragraph 1, do you find any spiritual movements that are, at least very probably, being prompted in Kerr himself or in others? If so, indicate those movements and your reason for your opinion.
2. In paragraph 2, the same question.
3. In paragraph 3, the same question.
4. Do you think Ignatius's teaching on discernment of spirits offers some grounds for judging whether Kerr's three personal experiences are in some sense "authentic theophanies or merely subjective fantasies"? Explain briefly.

Reading (in step 4 of "Method"): *Commentary,* 60–63, 82–90, 99–121; "EN," 15–22

● *Case 12* ●

1. Jim has for several years been a member of a religious congregation. He has gotten along well enough and certainly loves the congregation and is enthusiastic about its apostolic work. One serious difficulty, however, showed up along the line; and, despite his goodwill and effort and prayer, this has gotten worse rather than better. He generally feels resentful and distrustful of those in authority, and frequently his spontaneous first response to any directive or even suggestion from his superiors is rebellious. His efforts to be open and obedient put him under constant tension. Worse yet, he finds that even his attitude toward God is often tinged with fear and distrust. He is disturbed and

confused by all this, feels guilty and discouraged about ever growing into a truly Christlike man.

2.   He shares his problem with George, another young man in his group. (He cannot bring himself to be open with his superior.) His companion has been reading the Ignatian rules for discernment of spirits. He reads rules I, 2 and 4, to Jim and they decide that when Jim experiences rebelliousness, he is having a spiritual desolation, prompted by the evil spirit. So many of the signs mentioned by Ignatius are present. It will, therefore, go away, they think, if in accord with Ignatius's rules I, 6–8, Jim is patient and prays, does penance and goes against his antagonism to authority by being more-than-ordinarily submissive to his religious superiors.

3.   The problem does not disappear. One day, during an especially bad reaction to a superior's decision, Jim decides that it is best for him to leave the congregation. He impulsively packs up and leaves without a word to anyone.

4.   Afterwards, he experiences considerable satisfaction in having made his own decision and acted on it. This he takes for a spiritual consolation confirming his decision to leave the congregation. On the other hand, he feels rather anxious most of the time during the weeks after leaving, anxious, lonely, and guilty. This he takes for a spiritual desolation and a sign that he made a wrong choice in leaving. He is completely confused by these conflicting signs, and wonders whether Ignatian discernment of spirits is not really worthless.

5.   After a while, he finds that his initiative and intelligence enable him to get along well in the business world. He gets a position where he is his own boss. He makes friends, has a feeling of euphoria about life, and thanks God for all these gifts.

➤   *Questions for Reflection (in step 3 of "Method")*

1.   What do you think of Jim's feelings described in paragraph 1? Are they spiritual or nonspiritual or both? Explain.

2.   In paragraph 2, what do you think of Jim's seeking help from George? What do you think of the interpretation of Jim's experience reached by George and Jim? And what do you think of the way of overcoming Jim's bad attitude that they decide upon?

3.   What do you think of Jim's decision, in paragraph 3, to leave the congregation?

4.   What could you say to clear up Jim's confusion, described in paragraph 4, caused by the experiences that he sees as conflict-

ing evidence regarding the rightness or wrongness of his decision to leave the religious community?

5. In paragraph 5, do you understand Jim's euphoria and his gratitude to God as spiritual consolation?

Reading (in step 4 of "Method"): *Commentary,* 47–63, 103–15, 141–43, 198–204; "EN," 11–22, 25f.

● *Case 13* ●

[The story in this case appeared in the *Detroit Free Press,* Monday, August 26, 1985, 11 A. It is an excerpt from John De Lorean's book, *De Lorean* (Grand Rapids, Mich.: Zondervan Publishing House, 1985). Some deletions have been made and paragraph numbers inserted. It is an account of his experience while in prison.]

1. So, my first concern was getting a lawyer and my second concern was trying to understand what had happened to me. To aid me in the latter, I asked my wife Cristina to bring me a Bible. I began to read it. There is no doubt that this began my pilgrimage to understanding.

2. The most important person I met [in prison] was a young man who was one of the guards. He was working his way through seminary and was on duty from late afternoon until around midnight. He had a missionary zeal and had organized a Bible-study group for those prisoners who were interested. He asked me if I would like to attend, and I indicated that I would. This young man's training and enthusiasm made even what I had thought were fairly simple stories, such as the Old Testament one about Jonah and the whale, take on new life and depth. He told me Jesus loved me; he repeated this over and over again with many scriptural proofs.

3. I made the Bible the focus of my daily activities. During the ten days I was held in prison, there were three reasons for this. First, I had nothing else to do and this seemed to be an ideal way to pass the time; second, I had an intense and growing curiosity about God and needed to find answers; and third, I was finding that everything I had valued, everything I had thought I understood, was no longer clear. Without a doubt something was wrong in my life.

4. I was angry, frustrated, and scared. If I thought I was out of control before the arrest, now I was no longer in charge of anything. My strength, my "steel trap" mind, my arrogance and pride, all meant nothing.

5. The only pleasures I had were from the one-hour volleyball game I enjoyed with my fellow inmates each day and my intense study

of the Bible. In fact I found myself reading, thinking, and praying from 6:30 in the morning until it was time to turn out the lights at night.

6. In addition to my personal study, the young seminarian who was so determined to help those of us willing to listen, assisting us to understand the Bible, the Word of God, would visit me each day he could. In a simple manner he talked with me about Jesus Christ, the Son of God, telling me the story of his life on earth as a man and his death that was a once-and-for-all payment for the sins of mankind.

7. As he spoke, I came to the slow realization of how wrong my past had been. Who I had been did not matter. My money, my success or lack of it, my business reputation—all these superficial values were meaningless. I did not have to be special to obtain God's love.

8. This message was so simple. It was also a little frightening. I had spoken glibly of Christianity for many years without truly letting myself be open to Christ as a person I could know, as the Son of God who was my personal savior. I had always felt that being a Christian meant acting in a special manner to earn his love somehow. At the same time, I had been so arrogant: I wanted to be in charge of my life. I was the classic example of a person who saw himself as "captain of his fate and master of his soul." And hadn't I done a great job of it! Of course, the reality was that I never had to do it alone. God was there all the time. I had just refused to reach out and let him give me what is available to all of us if we only ask.

9. I have thought about the term "born again." I had never seen myself as a sinner or a bad man. I thought of myself as honest. I had never viciously tried to hurt anyone, and I had frequently gone out of my way to help others. I often gave and never asked for anything in return.

10. Everything I said sounded right and made my motives seem pure and good, but deep down inside I was really doing it all for myself. For John De Lorean. I was living a lie. I was an egomaniac, out of control.

11. I sat in my cell hour after hour, reflecting, understanding, and seeking forgiveness as I came to see myself for what I really was. For the first time in my life I was ready to stop playing the control game. I was ready to stop insisting on myself, my strengths, my desires. I was going to turn control of my life over to the Lord and let him lead instead of having the arrogance to try to make my own way, expecting God to follow. For the first time in my life, I was truly ready to follow Christ, no matter what that would mean, no matter where that would take me. I was a broken man, struck down, a humbled man with no place to turn.

12.   When the essence of this finally got through to me, I was stand-
ing in my cell with the Bible open on the upper bunk. I alternately read
and reflected upon my life, truly repentant for where I had failed and
determined to change. For the first time in my life, I was open to the
Lord. And then I felt his presence.

13.   A powerful warming embrace engulfed my body from the soles
of my feet to the top of my head. I was a man chilled from the elements, but suddenly wrapped in a comforting robe of strength and
light. I was filled with a sense of being loved, protected, at peace. I saw
no one, heard nothing, yet I knew at the very center of my existence
that everything would be all right. I knew Jesus was talking to me,
comforting me, telling me everything would be fine; the trial, my family
pressures, the life I had yet to lead would all work out in ways I could
not yet grasp. I felt healed, safe, protected from evil if I would just
continue the rest of my life's journey walking hand in hand with Christ.
I had been given a freedom of the soul that the steel bars of my cell,
the power of my accusers, and the greed of my corporate detractors
could never capture or destroy. In the depths of my despair, I had been
wrapped in a blanket of spiritual light and I would never be the same.

14.   Did this embrace last five minutes or twenty-five? I have no idea.
Time was meaningless. Eventually, I was again alone in my cell, yet not
alone. Safe. At peace. Filled with the love of Christ I had refused to
accept for too many years. Happiness and relief overwhelmed my body.
I felt physically drained, but my mind glowed in a new light.

15.   Then for the first time in years I began to cry, softly at first, then
racked with deep sobbing. After almost sixty years of arrogance and
pride, of trying to be in control, I had finally accepted the love of God
that had always been mine for the taking, regardless of success, failure,
triumph, or tragedy. Everything was going to be fine. I need never fear
again. And I have not.

16.   I was still in jail. I still had the ordeal of a criminal trial to face.
My company was still destroyed. But none of that mattered now. By
giving control of my life to the Lord, I had taken a major step forward; I
had gained new life that no amount of personal striving could ever have
achieved for me. And then I slept. Deep, restful sleep, warm with the
inner glow of the Lord.

➤   *Questions for Reflection (in step 3 of "Method")*

Show how one or more of the Ignatian rules for discernment of
spirits apply to what is said

1. in paragraphs 1 to 11
2. in paragraphs 12 and 13

3. in paragraphs 14 to 16

Reading (in step 4 of "Method"): *Commentary,* 47–70, 95–115: "EN,"
14–16, 19–21, 26f., 28f.

• *Case 14* •

[The following narrative in the first person is taken from Thérèse of
Lisieux, *The Story of a Soul,* translated by John Clark, O.C.D. (Washing-
ton, D.C.: Institute of Carmelite Studies, 1975), 210–14. The text is
somewhat condensed and paragraph numbers are added. Throughout,
Thérèse addresses her account to the Mother Prioress, who had induced
her to write it.]

1.   Dear Mother, you know well that God has deigned to make me
pass through many types of trials. I have suffered very much since I was
on earth; but if in my childhood I suffered with sadness, it is no longer
in this way that I suffer. It is with joy and peace. I am truly happy to
suffer. O Mother, you must know all the secrets of my soul in order not
to smile when you read these lines, for is there a soul less tried than my
own if one judges by appearances? Ah! if the trial I am suffering for a
year now appeared to the eyes of anyone, what astonishment would it
afford the observer!

2.   [Until this trial began] I was enjoying such a living faith, such a
clear *faith,* that the thought of heaven made up all my happiness. . . .
He [now] permitted my soul to be invaded by the thickest darkness,
and the thought of heaven, up until then so sweet to me, was no longer
anything but the cause of struggle and torment. This trial was to last
not a few days or a few weeks; it was not to be extinguished until the
hour set by God himself, and that hour has not yet come. I would like
to be able to express what I feel, but alas! I believe this is impossible.
One would have to travel through this dark tunnel to understand its
darkness. I will try to explain it by a comparison.

3.   I imagine I was born in a country that is covered in thick fog. I
never had the experience of contemplating the joyful appearance of
nature flooded and transformed by the brilliance of the sun. It is true
that from childhood I have heard people speak of these marvels; and I
know the country in which I am living is not really my true fatherland,
and there is another I must long for without ceasing. This is not simply
a story invented by someone living in the sad country where I am, but it
is a reality; for the King of the fatherland of the bright sun actually
came and lived for thirty-three years in the land of darkness. Alas! the
darkness did not understand that this divine King was the Light of the
world. . . .

4.   . . . the certainty of going away one day far from the sad and dark country had been given me from the day of my childhood. I did not believe it only because I heard it from persons much more knowledgeable than I, but I felt in the bottom of my heart real longings for this most beautiful country. Just as the genius of Christopher Columbus gave him a presentiment of a new world when nobody had even thought of such a thing, so also I felt that another land would one day serve me as a permanent dwelling place. Then suddenly the fog that surrounds me becomes more dense; it penetrates my soul and envelops it in such a way that it is impossible to discover within it the sweet image of my fatherland; everything has disappeared! When I want to rest my heart fatigued by the darkness surrounding it by recalling the memory of the luminous country after which I aspire, my torment redoubles; it seems to me that the darkness, borrowing the voice of sinners, says mockingly to me: "You are dreaming about the light, about a fatherland embalmed in the sweetest perfumes; you are dreaming about the *eternal* possession of the Creator of all these marvels; you believe that one day you will walk out of this fog which surrounds you! Advance, advance; rejoice in death that will give you not what you hope for but a night still more profound, the night of nothingness." . . . I don't want to write any longer about it; I fear I might blaspheme; I fear even that I have already said too much.

5.   Ah! may Jesus pardon me if I have caused him any pain, but he knows very well that while I do not have the *joy of faith,* I am trying to carry out its works at least. I believe I have made more acts of faith in this past year than all through my whole life. At each new occasion of combat, when my enemy provokes me, I conduct myself bravely. . . . I run towards my Jesus. I tell him I am ready to shed my blood to the last drop to profess my faith in the existence of *heaven.*

6.   I tell him, too, I am happy not to enjoy this beautiful heaven on this earth so that he will open it for all eternity to poor unbelievers. Also, in spite of this trial which has taken away *all my joy,* I can nevertheless cry out: *"You have given me DELIGHT, O Lord, in ALL Your doings."* For is there a greater joy than that of suffering out of love for you? . . . But if my suffering was really unknown to you, which is impossible, I would still be happy to have it, if through it I could prevent or make reparation for one single sin against *faith.*

7.   My dear Mother, I may perhaps appear to you to be exaggerating my trial. In fact, if you are judging according to the sentiments I express in my little poems composed this year, I must appear to you as a soul filled with consolations and one for whom the veil of faith is almost torn aside; and yet it is no longer a veil for me, it is a wall that reaches right up to the heavens and over the starry firmament. When I

sing of the happiness of heaven and of the eternal possession of God, I feel no joy in this, for I sing simply what I WANT [will?] TO BELIEVE. It is true that at times a very small ray of the sun comes to illumine my darkness, and then the trial ceases for an *instant,* but afterwards the memory of this ray, instead of causing me joy, makes my darkness even more dense.

8. Never have I felt before this, dear Mother, how sweet and merciful the Lord really is, for he did not send me this trial until the moment I was capable of bearing it. A little earlier I believe it would have plunged me into a state of discouragement. Now it is taking away everything that could be a natural satisfaction in my desire for heaven. Dear Mother, it seems to me now that nothing could prevent me from flying away, for I no longer have any great desires except that of loving to the point of dying of love.

June 9

➤ *Questions for Reflection (in step 3 of "Method")*

1. In paragraphs 2 to 4 and 7, Thérèse describes her experience of desolation. Is this what Ignatius means by a spiritual desolation or a nonspiritual one? Explain.

2. It is clear from paragraphs 5 to 8 that Thérèse did not actually decline in faith, hope, and charity and never actually yielded to discouragement. Does this fact call into question that she was really experiencing a spiritual desolation? Explain why it does or does not.

3. In paragraphs 1 and 6, Thérèse seems to be saying that during her desolation and even on account of it, she is delighted and joyful. She seems to be experiencing consolation while in desolation. This is very confusing. Can you make sense of it?

4. What Ignatian rule is illustrated by paragraph 8?

Reading (in step 4 of "Methods"): *Commentary,* 120f., 127–44, 177f., 182–91; "EN," 15f., 21f., 24, 25f.

● *Case 15* ●

[This case was written by a student in spiritual theology. Let us call her Adele.]

1. I am a forty-three-year-old religious Sister from an English-speaking culture, living in a community whose language and culture are French. I was a school teacher until five years ago. Then my provincial asked me to consider adult religious education as a ministry. I am involved in this work since then. I enjoy it very much.

2. In addition to the tensions from work, I have for many years experienced a restlessness and an inner confusion that at times I could not identify. I have always felt sure of my vocation to the religious life. However, I have continually questioned whether I was in the congregation God wanted me to be in. I feel very limited by the French culture and language. I have never succeeded in making it my own. Moreover, there are very few possibilities to be with other English-speaking Sisters and to do ministry in English. Besides all that, I have also during this time experienced a deep desire to spend more time in prayer and solitude. At times I wondered if God might be calling me to a contemplative way of life.

3. Although I was in great inner conflict, I feared telling anyone how I really felt about belonging to the community or the tensions I suffered when I was expected to speak French. And I certainly preserved secrecy about my desire for solitude and prayer. In fact, I kept many things secret for fear of what others might think of me.

4. As time went on I could no longer live with this tension. So I went to see a priest for direction. This priest was also a psychological counselor. In fact, I came to realize that he knew little or nothing about discernment of spirits; he did, however, help me psychologically.

5. I received counseling for about two years, not frequently but on an ongoing basis. I believed I was becoming more myself. I explored my inner feelings and became more aware of psychological limitations. However, confusion about my future continued. I often wondered if this might be a call from God. The director suggested I not look at it until I had completed counseling.

6. Gradually I began to become depressed. I didn't know what was happening to me. I was discouraged with myself. I felt God was totally absent from my life. As the months went on, I felt that God didn't care about me now and he probably didn't care about my future. I tried to pray, but it seemed impossible and useless. So, I prayed less and gave up on any examination of what was going on in my life from a spiritual perspective; I was altogether taken up with examination from a psychological point of view.

7. The times were not always characterized by desolation. They were intermingled with periods of longing for God and feeling joy in the presence of God. The consoling experiences rarely came at times set apart for prayer.

8. Finally I felt moved to do more spiritual reading. I read Scripture, the writings of Teresa of Avila, and a book by William Johnston. I received great peace from these readings. One day I read Isa. 43:1. I was touched by the words "You are mine." The depression (as I then

called it) left me. I felt at peace; I had a deep sense of God's presence, his nearness, his love for me, his providence. I had never before experienced God so deeply.

9. I had, during the time of desolation, been tempted to withdraw from a summer theology program that I had begun. Now, however, since the issue of my future in the community continued to recur and always with more intensity, I decided to look into this issue during my studies in the coming summer. I chose the courses that I thought would be helpful: apostolic spirituality, theology of the Spiritual Exercises with the nineteenth-annotation retreat, and the course on discernment. I prepared for this through my prayer.

10. I began a discernment of God's will according to the Ignatian method. I noticed that underlying all the advantages I adverted to for remaining in rather than transferring from my community was a self-centered fear rather than any positive drawing to greater service of God. I finally concluded that I was called to transfer to another community. I was very much at peace with that.

11. I then tried another discernment process to decide which community I should enter. Here I felt blocked. It seemed impossible to go any further. I had a sense God was no longer with me in this process. I was tired, discouraged, and again ready to give up on everything. I wondered why I had returned to the program this summer. I thought maybe God didn't care about my future. I might never find his will for me. I was tempted to shorten prayer and skip liturgy. I felt lost and alone in my struggle. I was utterly confused.

12. Remembering what I had been learning from the course on Ignatian discernment made all the difference now. I took the following actions: more prayer and reflection (rule I, 6); more acts of faith that God always loves me and stands by me, in desolation as well as in consolation, no matter how I feel (rule I, 7); determination to be patient (rule I, 8); resisting the evil spirit boldly and confidently (rule I, 12). As a result of these actions, instead of panic I felt some inner strength, some calm underneath all the pain and confusion, some ability to step outside it and carry on with hope.

13. I also remembered rule I, 13, and decided to ask for help. The one to whom I went for help was very warm, understanding, and insightful. She helped me to reflect on what was happening. She asked me if I knew how transfers were made. My director explained that I must make a personal discernment; but since I am a member of a community, it must be a mutual discernment. She advised me to discuss the matter with the authorities in my community rather than bringing to them a finalized decision. I recognized the truth of what she said. My

depression lifted. I could talk about the matter without crying. I felt supported by God. I was more energetic. I felt deep peace and was inclined to pray. I felt close to God at prayer and more sensitive to the needs of others. I am surprised now to see how free I feel about accepting whatever God might reveal to me concerning the future.

➤ *Question for Reflection (in step 3 of "Method")*

As you go through this case paragraph by paragraph, beginning with paragraph 2, show how the Ignatian rules are of help for understanding what is going on in Adele and what is appropriate or inappropriate in her ways of responding to the movements she experiences.

Reading (in step 4 of "Method"): *Commentary,* 56–73, 109–15, 127–38, 141–43, 148–81. "EN," 14–16, 21–24

●   *Case 16*   ●

[This is an account given by one who knew the person called Dorothy in this case and helped her through this experience.]

1.   Dorothy is seventy-two years old, a widow of thirty years, a traditional and devout Catholic. She visits patients in a local hospital (or in their homes if she knows them) and daily visits her "friends" at one of the local rest homes. Her daily routine also includes Mass, morning and evening prayer, and a forty-five-minute period of meditation after Mass.

2.   Despite her basic good will, Dorothy easily and frequently has feelings of anger, impatience, and resentment. She goes to confession often; her confessions, while sincere, are always the same. Each time, after she receives the sacrament of reconciliation, Dorothy feels a peace and joy and eagerness both to pray and to minister to others.

3.   Invariably, in a conversation with a hospital patient, one of the elderly, or even a neighbor, something again happens that evokes spiteful feelings in her. These feelings grow until she can't face visiting anymore. She feels hypocritical, unlovable, and incapable of love; she decides to stop her visiting. However, she keeps up her prayer, telling herself that if she prays hard enough and persistently enough, the Lord will take away these bad feelings. Finally, she goes to confession again, enumerates her sins, receives absolution, and begins the cycle all over again.

4.   Once, however, when Dorothy had been reclusive for a longer time than usual, praying and waiting for her negative feelings to go away, she found that she only became more irritable and frustrated with herself and with God too. She felt that God had simply written her off because she could not correct herself. She decided to stop going to Mass daily, because she felt totally unworthy to receive the Eucharist.

5.   Sister Angela, who works with the elderly in Dorothy's parish, noticed that Dorothy had stopped coming to daily Mass. She also noticed that Dorothy had apparently given up her visiting for a particularly long time. She went to see Dorothy at her apartment. Dorothy was so happy to see her that she spent most of the visit crying. Sister Angela convinced Dorothy that she should begin regular meetings with her for spiritual direction. Dorothy began a serious dialogue with Sister Angela on the whole process that had been going on in her. Even though spontaneous feelings of anger, jealousy and impatience continued to arise in her, she came to recognize, with Angela's help, that the inclination to cease from visiting and from going to Mass and Communion was not the answer to her problem. She also began to experience much less frustration and discouragement.

➤   *Question for Reflection (in step 3 of "Method")*

Paragraph by paragraph, how would you apply the Ignatian rules in order to understand each step of Dorothy's experience?

Reading (in step 4 of "Method"): *Commentary,* 56–68, 125–44, 147–64, 198–204: "EN," 14–17, 21–24, 25f.

•   *Case 17*   •

[This case is taken from an article in the *Michigan Catholic* newspaper, December 2, 1977, pp. 1 and 7. It is condensed and the paragraphing is changed. Paragraph numbers are inserted for facilitating reference to them. This story is told mostly in the words of Marietta Jaeger, whose seven-year-old daughter, Susie, was kidnapped and murdered. The story begins after the kidnapping and before Mrs. Jaeger knew that Susie had been murdered.]

1.   At the end of one long day in which I had found each of my children alone and crying and seen the pain and anguish in my husband's heart, I felt drained and I said angrily, "I could kill that man for what he has done to my family." Instead, God gave me the grace to desire to do his will and I asked only three things of him: to help me learn to forgive the man with my lips and love him with my heart; to allow me to be part of the resolution when Susie was found; and if something had happened to her, to help me to understand why he had allowed it to happen.

2.   When this first happened, I thought Satan had caused it and that God would now rescue Susie. But now I thought, if God is God, he could have stopped this. But he didn't. What kind of God would allow this? What had Susie ever done? Maybe there isn't a God. Maybe after

all he is only a psychological crutch. I really wrestled with this, and I knew I had to resolve it. It was tearing me apart. Did I believe in God?

3.   I was alone in my bedroom at the time, when suddenly I felt as if somebody reached over and pulled me onto safe ground. I began to pray and pray, made a commitment to God, and he came to me. I felt as if I was absolutely surrounded, almost a physical feeling of love of God. It was incredible. I couldn't believe anyone could love me that much. I found him absolutely irresistible, and I had no choice but to love and serve him.

[Marietta prayed for the grace to forgive the kidnapper. A year after the kidnapping, the kidnapper contacted Marietta by phone and talked for an hour. While he was talking, she experienced "a shower of love and forgiveness." Overcome by her loving and forgiving attitude, he broke down and sobbed in anguish. Several times after that, Marietta was in contact with the man by phone or in person and came to actually love as well as pity him deeply; she only wanted to have him get the psychiatric help he needed. (He had committed several other similar crimes.) Finally, he was apprehended by the police, made a full confession, and then committed suicide. Marietta's response was a surprising and touching one.]

4.   This was not what I wanted for him. I felt as much grief at his suicide as at losing Susie. I've learned that God does indeed give us the power to live by his laws of love and forgiveness; I am the first to tell you that that is not always easy. I loved the man who killed her—and that's only the work of God, no credit to me.

➤ *Question for Reflection (in step 3 of "Method")*

Applying the Ignatian rules for discernment of spirits, what spirit or spirits do you find affecting Marietta Jaeger in each of the foregoing paragraphs?

Reading (in step 4 of "Method"): *Commentary,* 56–69, 127–38, 160–62: "EN," 14–16, 21f., 25f.

● *Case 18* ●

1.   In her earlier years, Rose Ellen had worked as a secretary in the chancery and lived a devout life. She participated in the sacramental life of the Church. Every day she prayed the Liturgy of the Hours, attended the Eucharist, and spent time in meditative prayer. She cared for her two children, the fruit of a marriage that had ended in divorce; and she did some evangelizing work for the parish. She was a woman of intelligence, efficient and full of drive.

2.   The signs of maturing spirituality in her life collapsed when she was let go from her job as a secretary in the chancery—unjustly, so she thought, and in an unkindly manner. At that time she felt deeply hurt, humiliated, rejected, and very angry at the priest who had been her boss. In fact, her anger expanded: she became bitter and cynical about the clergy in general; she directed these feelings about the clergy toward God and the Church. What had been a relationship of intimacy with the Lord was no longer so. She felt dry and empty and abandoned even by him. She adopted a "who cares?" attitude: "If this is what I get after years of faithful service at great cost to myself, I quit." And quit she did. She stopped praying, withdrew from her work of evangelization, and discontinued her practices of piety.

3.   After a long time, Rose Ellen finally went to someone for spiritual counseling and was able, by God's grace, to overcome her resentment and begin to live again a life of prayer and service of God's people. She is now in her fifties. She feels called to seek out women who have given up their faith because of experiences that alienated them from the Church. Rose Ellen's commitment to this ministry had grown out of her own experience. The women she meets with are often divorced or separated, living alone with the responsibility of raising families on their own. Some of them are victims of domestic violence. Most of them are unchurched women who had been practicing Catholics.

➤ *Questions for Reflection (in step 3 of "Method")*

1.   Depending on paragraph 1, before Rose Ellen's crisis, would rule I, 1 or 2, seem to apply to her?

2.   Using the Ignatian rules for discernment of spirits, can you cast light on the account in paragraph 2?

3.   Does Rose Ellen's response to being fired call for some change from or addition to your answer to question 1?

4.   Do you think of any advice based on the Ignatian rules that Rose Ellen needed at the time of her crisis?

5.   Does paragraph 3 suggest any addition to rule I, 9, another reason, beyond those suggested by St. Ignatius, why God might have allowed Rose Ellen to go through her painful desolation and experience of alienation before being healed?

Reading (in step 4 of "Method"): *Commentary,* 47–77, 127–38, 141–43; "EN," 14–17, 21f.

● *Case 19* ●

[The following case is taken from Hannah W. Smith, *The Christian's Secret of a Happy Life* (New York: Ballantine Books, 1986), 98. The author tells of a woman (let us call her Sadie) who]

had been living very happily in the life of faith for some time, and had been so free from temptations as almost to begin to think she would never be tempted again. But suddenly a very peculiar form of temptation had assailed and horrified her. She found that the moment she began to pray, dreadful thoughts of all kinds would rush into her mind. She had lived a very sheltered, innocent life; and these thoughts seemed so awful to her that she felt she must be one of the most wicked of sinners to be capable of having them. She began by thinking that she could not possibly have entered into the rest of faith and ended by concluding that she had never even been born again. Her soul was in an agony of distress.

➤ *Question for Reflection (in step 3 of "Method")*

What Ignatian rules would enable Sadie to understand and deal with the feelings and thoughts that she was experiencing? Explain.

Reading (in step 4 of "Method"): *Commentary,* 37f., 127–38, 177f., 185–91; "EN," 14–16, 21f., 24, 25f.

● *Case 20* ●

1.　Alice, a young Christian woman was recently married. She and her husband moved to a small town where she joined the local parish community. Previously she had been very active in her home parish, especially in the youth group and music-ministry group. She hoped to participate in these or similar ways in her new parish. She has continued to be very faithful in her daily reading of the Scriptures and prayer and has found much joy and peace in the Lord. She hoped also to be able to find others in the parish community who would be interested in sharing their faith and prayer and bringing life to the whole parish.

2.　Alice's former parish had been a very active community, where she experienced great support and encouragement from the pastoral team, as also from other members of the community. After only a few weeks in her new parish, she realized that the situation was very different. The pastor seemed uninterested in any ordinary parish worship or activity except for the half-hour Sunday Mass, with virtually no lay participation. Although the community seemed reverent and sincere, no one seemed to realize that his or her religious expression of the faith could be more meaningful and inspiring.

3. Even in what seemed to be a hopeless situation, however, Alice decided that she wanted to become actively involved in her Christian community and felt that the Lord was calling her to influence and help others to grow in their faith and their relationship with Jesus. She longed for others to experience the joy she found in the Lord. Gradually she found others who were interested in becoming involved in some ways and discovered also that the pastor was somewhat open to her services and leadership.

4. After a year, however, with only minimal progress and a number of disputes with the pastor, Alice sees herself as a pretty complete failure and feels altogether discouraged about achieving any growth in the parish. Recently, even in her own personal prayer, she has experienced feelings of emptiness, of being abandoned by God. She feels that God is no longer near and she becomes overwhelmed with frustration. She wonders if she isn't altogether losing her faith in God's loving care. She does continue to be faithful to community worship and to her own personal times for prayer, but it all seems hopeless and meaningless.

5. She begins to think it was a foolish decision to become involved, and finally decides she will withdraw from her involvement and so escape the tension and frustration she has been experiencing.

➤ *Questions for Reflection (in step 3 of "Method")*

1. Is it rule I, 1, or I, 2, that applies to Alice?
2. In paragraphs 4 and 5, which Ignatian rules would help understand what is going on within Alice?
3. What rules would give her good guidance if she understood them during this critical time?

Reading (in step 4 of "Method"): *Commentary,* 47–54, 57–59, 72–77, 127–43; "EN," 14–17, 21–24, 25–29

● *Case 21* ●

[This case is an account of a spiritual experience over an extended period by one whom we will call Susan. She is a laywoman, trained for ministry as a retreat director and working in a diocesan retreat house. The account is in her own words for the most part.]

1. I intend in the presentation of this case to review the movements in my spiritual life during the past months. I choose this particular time segment because of the diversity of motions in it and, most of all, because I want to deepen my insight into it so as to surrender myself more to the action of the Holy Spirit within me.

2.   From October through December I felt close to the Lord in both prayer and ministry. Over the course of these months, I was given additional administrative responsibilities, which I enthusiastically undertook, and welcomed the appreciative remarks concerning my work. Prayer at this time was refreshingly inviting: I found it easy to be still before the Lord and bask in his love.

3.   In January my apostolate intensified. The weight of added responsibilities drove me to prayer. However, I was unable in prayer to divest myself of the hectic pace of the day: it became increasingly more difficult to engage in the still prayer to which I was accustomed. Although the Lord seemed to grow more distant in prayer, his presence in the retreat work I was engaged in was unmistakable. Witnessing numerous individuals, young and old alike, touched by the Gospel served to strengthen my faith.

4.   Come February, though my work changed once again, I maintained the same harried pace, only with a more noticeable toll upon my prayer life. For the succeeding four months, I can recall no more than five prayer times in which I experienced an ease at being before the Lord. Prayer time became fraught with restlessness, anxiety, and aloneness. I would begin with trying to still myself and focus on God, and end either falling asleep or battling innumerable distractions and temptations.

5.   My resolve to remain faithful to prayer weakened. Finally, I became so discouraged about prayer that I began to shorten it in the hope of retaining more peace of mind. Gradually I found myself tending toward confusion and discouragement about living a life of faith, hope, and love. Unfortunately, I did not share this with my spiritual director, choosing instead to speak about the apparent success of the ministry. (Curiously, throughout this time span, the fruits of the apostolate remained rich.)

6.   With the coming of summer, the time approached for my annual retreat. With mixed feelings I took time out to "get this over with" by making the directed Spiritual Exercises at another retreat house. The retreat schedule was a welcome change of pace. It easily permitted prayer, Mass, exercise, regular meals, and sleep. All this brought relaxation and tranquility for reflection. During the First Week I was given the painful insight that activity had become the source for protecting and maintaining a "superwoman" image. What had begun for the greater service of God had turned into greater self-seeking. With this insight came peace and thereafter a growing sense of Christ's love for me. Nearly every day I was surprised and gladdened by the numerous and varied ways the Lord manifested himself to me. The director of

the Exercises was helpful in planning how to combine prayer and action and even in understanding how to become contemplative in action.

➤ *Question for Reflection (in step 3 of "Method")*

Applying the Ignatian rules for the discernment of spirits, how would you, paragraph by paragraph, interpret each step of Susan's experience?

Reading (in step 4 of "Method"): *Commentary,* 39–41, 56–69, 115–21, 127f., 143f., 249f., 253–56; "EN," 13f., 15–17, 21f., 27–29

● *Case 22* ●

[Sister Jane is in her late thirties. She is an introverted but affectionate personality, having a lively imagination and a wide range of feelings that can be easily moved by idealism and enthusiasm and just as easily downcast by failure and loneliness. She loves Christ and desires to grow in her nearness to God and in service to others. For the past year and a half she has been under spiritual direction and has come to a deepening of her inner life through a daily hour of prayer and monthly days of recollection. Presently she has come to a retreat center to make an eight-day directed retreat under her own spiritual director. Below is a description of the day-by-day progress of the retreat.]

Day 1: Jane begins the retreat in peace, with a quiet expectation of meeting Christ. She reflects, as directed, on chapter 55 of Isaiah and is attracted to verse 1: "All you who are thirsty, come to the water!" and verse 12: "Yes, in joy you shall depart, in peace you shall be brought back." She is confident that the Lord will nourish and refresh her for her ministry.

Day 2: In praying over the assigned Scripture verse, "Come to me . . . I will refresh you" (Matt. 11:28), Jane experiences an inner cleansing and refreshment as if she were drawn into a fountain of fire and water. She is filled with wonder and joy. The blissful feeling remains with her throughout the day, and she experiences the nearness of Jesus as she ponders other assigned Scripture readings and listens to what the Lord is saying to her.

Day 3: She arises early next morning quietly hoping for similar experiences of the Lord. She prays over the assigned section of the Canticle of Canticles and experiences a sweet joy at the thought of the Lord's love for her. She then decides to prolong her praying periods from an hour to an hour and a half each so as to become more immersed in Christ. She does not inform her director about this plan. She spends seven hours that day in prayer. Her excitement grows. That night she cannot fall asleep.

Day 4: Jane gets up with a bad headache, feeling exhausted and under strain. She cannot pray well. All joy has evaporated. She is tired and sad and moody. Finally in the evening she tells the director about her action of the previous day and its results. The director advises cutting down on prayer time and resting more.

Day 5: She follows the advice, prays less but still has no enthusiasm and is filled with gloom.

Day 6: At her morning prayer she becomes very much disturbed. She begins to doubt the Lord's presence to her even in the opening days of the retreat. Probably, she thinks, she should attribute everything to her overactive imagination. Who is she to be given a taste of the sweetness of the Lord? She begins to grow discouraged at the thought that she is not meant for a deep prayer life. Her desire for God is just an illusion. The rest of the day is one of disquietude, confusion, and a sense of discouragement.

Day 7: The director urges her to trust her earlier experiences and to hope in the Lord that he will bring good even from this desolation. She directs her to pray over John 14, especially the opening verses, "Do not let your hearts be troubled." She prays quietly over the passages, rests more, takes walks in the garden.

Day 8: On the closing day she returns to chapter 55 of Isaiah: "Come to the water . . . in joy you shall depart." A calm settles on her mind and spirit. She knows that she is loved by God. She also knows at her deepest level that the experience of the second day was genuine. She has become more aware of her weaknesses, especially her undisciplined imagination and her rapidly fluctuating emotions. She prays for light and strength to manage these and become more balanced emotionally. She ends the retreat in quiet gratitude. She looks forward now in hope to her ministry—a more wise and serene woman.

➤ *Question for Reflection (in step 3 of "Method")*

What Ignatian rules for discernment of spirits apply to the experiences of each day during Jane's retreat? Explain.

Reading (in step 4 of "Method"): *Commentary,* 47–78, 95–115, 125–27, 141–43, 155–204, 222–43; "EN," 14–17, 21–26, 27–29

● **Case 23** ●

[The author of this case is a woman who is experienced and successful in directing retreats. Let us call her Kathy. She is relating her own experience. As she assured me, "This is fact, not fiction."]

1. During this past year I gave a series of preached retreats to the members of a religious congregation. I am frequently nervous before giving talks, but I was unusually so at the beginning of the first retreat. I brought my fear to God in prayer and meditated on the reasons I had for trust in him, no matter how things seemed. God gave me grace to be calm, do my best, and leave the consequences to him. From then on, all went well. I enjoyed giving the retreat and was grateful for the ways God worked in the retreatants and in me. It was during the next retreat that the real trouble began.

2. As the second retreat of the series began, I was unusually confident in myself. However, severe nervousness started again as I prepared to give the second talk. I began to think that this group was less receptive, that the material I had was no good, and so on. I wished I had stopped after the first retreat.

3. Before the third talk, panic set in. I found it almost impossible to prepare. When I began to pray it was scattered prayer. As I walked to the conference room, I felt a real heaviness and had to push myself to get there. I dismissed the positive feedback that I was getting, telling myself, They are just being kind. When I heard myself saying this, I labeled what was happening "temptation" and decided to pray Psalm 27 and to fast in preparation for the next talk.

4. Before the fourth talk the heaviness and dread increased to such a point that I felt physically ill. I began to think that God was trying to show me that I really was not cut out for retreat work. (I had been giving them for years.) I even considered how I might cancel the other retreats scheduled. There was a priest in the house who took care of liturgy and was available for confessions. I thought about going to talk with him but feared he would just laugh at me. As I interviewed retreatants, I was quick to point out the reasons to be grateful for what God was doing in them. It never dawned on me to do the same with my life.

5. After the fourth talk, I asked to talk with the priest, but was quick to add, "Of course, if you are busy . . ." He saw me right away. After asking some questions (and after hearing my confession), he said, "Isn't God good? See how he is protecting you from yourself. It isn't likely you'll get proud giving this retreat." As I went to give the fifth talk and felt nervous again, I recalled what the priest had said to me and I became deeply grateful for God's protective love. The nervousness left

and peace and joy took over. The rest of the retreat was fun! The following retreat was sheer grace. (There were thirty Sisters between the ages of seventy-eight and ninety-two. Ordinarily I would have been more than nervous.) I was so calm and joyful that the priest whom I had consulted asked to talk with me about his life. The calm persists and I am looking forward to future scheduled retreats.

➤ *Questions for Reflection (in step 3 of "Method")*

1. What spirits do you see working in paragraphs 1 and 2? Explain.

2. Would you characterize Kathy's experience in paragraph 3 as spiritual desolation? Why or why not?

3. Is there anything in the Ignatian rules that is clearly relevant to understanding and dealing with the experience described in paragraph 4?

4. In paragraph 5 what other rules do you see clearly illustrated?

Reading (in step 4 of "Method"): *Commentary*, 54–70, 127–38, 150–55, 198–204; "EN," 15f., 21–24, 25f.

● **Case 24** ●

1. Recently, I received a letter from a friend, Stan. He has been at his new job as vocation director for the diocese for about a year. He is a priest, living in a downtown parish near the chancery. At this time, there is considerable unrest in the diocese, and a number of Stan's friends are leaving the exercise of the priesthood.

2. In his letter, he says that in the vocation ministry, as in every job, once you have settled in there is more and more to be done. Under the pressure of things to be done, he has begun to omit personal prayer, to neglect the breviary sometimes, and to offer Mass without preparation. In fact, in reflecting over the past year, he is tempted to wonder whether he has really prayed at all during it. He knows very well, of course, that he has, but he is discouraged and confused. He used to feel that God loved him so much, prayer was so "comforting" then. Where is the Lord in all this? he wonders. Just when he needs God most, his prayer is empty, full of restlessness, dark and confused. He feels left alone by God to struggle without his help.

3. Lastly, he added, "Although I seem to be doing well as vocation director, maybe I should quit the job, since my decline in prayer life is coincidental with it and seems to result from it."

➤ *Questions for Reflection (in step 3 of "Method")*

What can be found in the Ignatian rules that could answer Stan's three questions:

1. Where is the Lord in all this?
2. Why isn't God more present to me, helping me?
3. Should I resign from my position as vocation director for the diocese?

Reading (in step 4 of "Method"): *Commentary,* 56–70, 122–44, 152–56, 182–91, 198f.; "EN," 14–16, 21–24, 25f.

SIX

PROPOSED RESPONSES TO THE QUESTIONS FOR REFLECTION

● *Responses to Questions for Case 1* ●

1. The evidence in this case all indicates that Carlo is predominantly a spiritually maturing person: He prays, goes to Mass, reflects on the Scripture reading and homily, and is saddened when it seems to him that God is absent from his life and that he is not growing into a really good Christian. However, like all the rest of us, he is no doubt spiritually unintegrated, has some antispiritual dispositions, some tendencies which reveal that in some dimensions of his life he is spiritually regressive. To be aware of these dispositions is necessary for understanding his experience.

2. In the light of the foregoing response to question 1, both rules (I, 1 and 2) can be applicable to Carlo. In the present case, rule I, 2, is more to the point.

3. As noted in response to question 1, Carlo prays, attends Mass, wants to understand the teaching of Holy Scripture, is deeply concerned about being in union with God, about being a good Christian and wants help to do so. All these facts indicate a living faith, faith that issues in love and hope. Since such faith is the radical effect of the Holy Spirit and is impossible without the Spirit's action, the movements flowing from it can reasonably be thought to be prompted by the Holy Spirit.

Carlo is experiencing spiritual desolation. He feels as if God is absent. Based on that feeling, he thinks that he must have turned away from God; as a consequence, he feels discouraged. All this is a clear sign of the influence of the evil spirit (*Commentary,* 57–60, 127–38).

There is no evident nonspiritual movement that is significant in this experience. However, such movements might appear if the conversation widens into consideration of his whole spiritual life and personality, as it would in ongoing spiritual direction. Thus, it might come to light that Carlo has a bad self-image, tends to be overly demanding of himself, has irrational guilt feelings, and so on. Such attitudes could well be an occasion for spiritual desolation even though they themselves are nonspiritual.

4. In light of rules I, 1f., 4f., and II, 7, and all that is said above in the responses to the first and third questions it is clear that Carlo is being moved by the Holy Spirit and by the evil spirit in conflicting ways.

5. Carlo could profit by having almost all the first set of rules for discernment of spirits explained to him. To begin with, he needs to understand all that is said in the foregoing responses to questions 1 to 4. Especially, right now, both he and the homilist whom he heard need to be disabused of the not uncommon but altogether false and harmful idea that passing feelings of spiritual peace and joy, contingent spiritual consolation, are *the* sign of the Holy Spirit's acting in one's life. He needs to understand that the radical sign of the Holy Spirit's presence and action in one's life is living faith (or love rooted in living faith), with or without spiritual consolation (peace and joy), and that among all other signs the most certain and necessary are courage and energy for living a life of Christian faith, hope, and love, with or without consolation.

• *Responses to Questions for Case 2* •

Before answering the questions for reflection, two matters of interpretation must be settled. I have found that some interpret what is said in this story in a different way than I do, consequently with different discernment of spirits. First, are we to understand that the young man really had kept the commandments from his earliest days or that he was making a false claim? Second, what was his reason for going away sorrowful? In my responses I am accepting the young man's claim as truthful. My main reason for doing so is that Jesus seems clearly to let it pass as true and continues to deal with him accordingly. I also understand that the young man was sad as he went away because deep down he wanted to come to Jesus and follow him but did not have the courage to give up his wealth.

1. The young man was predominantly disposed to go from good to better in God's service (rule I, 2). That was why he asked Jesus, "What must I do to inherit eternal life?" He had kept the commandments that Jesus mentioned and evidently was looking to do more than that. That is why Jesus then proposed an ideal that surpassed what he had yet done.

2. The young man is being moved in conflicting ways by the Holy Spirit and by the evil spirit. He is moved by the Holy Spirit to desire eternal life and to do what has to be done in order to inherit it. He is

moved by the evil spirit in accord with his disposition to remain wealthy and have the security, prestige, and power that wealth brings.

3. When discerning spirits, we have to go beyond the question whether the person is overall or predominantly spiritually maturing or regressing. After all, everyone has both good and evil dispositions and tendencies (*Commentary*, 72–77). We have to ask further, seeking to learn on what dimension of the person, on what disposition and tendency, the spirit is acting. Here it is the young man's attachment to wealth. The evil spirit would not make him sad about yielding to that disposition and turning way from Jesus; quite the contrary. It is the movement of the Holy Spirit that would conflict with that disposition and make the man disturbed and sad about yielding to it and refusing Jesus' invitation to be an intimate follower. We see, therefore, that the Holy Spirit is acting on two opposing dimensions of the young man's personality, two opposing dispositions, one which is in accord with the Holy Spirit and one which is in conflict with the movement of the Holy Spirit, namely, his inordinate attachment to wealth and fear of poverty.

●   *Responses to Questions for Case 3*   ●

1. Just as it is stated, this is a nonspiritual consolation: there is no evidence that my joy depends on living faith or of itself leads to an increase of such faith.

2. Nonspiritual desolation: there is no evidence that my negative mood of itself directly tends to diminish my Christian faith, hope, and love.

3. This is still nonspiritual desolation: my feeling hurt and sad is, in this instance, no more antispiritual than other things, such as sleepiness or a headache, that can hinder prayer and distract attention from the needs of others but do not of themselves directly tend to diminish living faith.

4. Now something antispiritual appears, something that of itself directly attacks living faith, tends to diminish or destroy it if not resisted. Therefore, this experience can be called a spiritual desolation.

5. Uncertain without further data: the setting would suggest that the delight is a spiritual consolation; but as we all know by experience, it is very easy even in a setting of religious worship for one to have a delightful aesthetic experience, one that does not depend on living faith or of itself tend to increase such faith.

6. If the statement ended after "I weep," the experience would remain uncertain, but would very likely be a spiritual consolation. What follows, however, leaves little doubt that the experience is a desolation; in fact, it is almost surely a spiritual desolation, attacking faith and

hope as it does. Still, one could take the statement to mean that I despair of my own goodness and effort and put all my hope in God alone. In that case, *if* the experience brought feelings of peace, it could be a spiritual consolation.

7. Nothing that is said here removes uncertainty about how to understand the experience. I could be happy because I see my brilliant performance as a gift of God, a sign of his love, and am happy because of faith in his love for me. If so, I am in spiritual consolation. But I could feel happy just because passing the exam improves my self-esteem and brings praise, or because it is a stepping stone to some self-centered goal I have in mind. Then the experience will be a nonspiritual consolation. My thanking God does not necessarily argue against the consolation being nonspiritual. I could be thanking God for the successful outcome, while my happy feelings are grounded not on faith in God's love for me but merely on the natural benefits that follow from my success. In that case, giving thanks to God is a spiritual movement but is not a spiritual consolation. Not every good spiritual movement is a spiritual consolation.

8. Uncertain: the ground of the joy is ambiguous. It could be the spiritual good I believe God has effected in those I work for or my faith in God's love for and providence over us. If so, this experience would be a spiritual consolation. On the other hand, the ground of my joy could be my sense of self-importance and the praise I receive for work well done. If so, the joy is not at all a spiritual consolation.

9. Again, the movement of thanks to God is a spiritual movement, arising from faith in God and his providential action in my life and the lives of others to whom I have ministered. But is it a spiritual *consolation*? Probably but not necessarily. Giving thanks to God very probably implies some peace and joy of a spiritual nature. But I can also give thanks to God when in dryness or even in spiritual desolation. So the interpretation of this statement as it stands must remain uncertain.

●   *Responses to Question for Case 4*   ●

We assume that John Woolman is predominantly disposed to go from good to better in God's service. Therefore, rule 2 applies. However, like all of us, he still has dispositions in conflict with his predominant attitude; insofar as he does, rule 1 can apply (*Commentary,* 72–78). In the experiences being described, Woolman is, as Penning de Vries says, "waging war within himself"—or rather, he is caught in a war being waged in him and over him by good and evil spirits.

In paragraph 1, Woolman is touched by the Holy Spirit in that dimension of his personality where he is disposed to avoid confrontation even with those who want him to do what is in conflict with his moral principles. As a consequence, he experiences, not spiritual consolation, but distress (*Commentary*, 74–77). After rationalizing, he does what he is asked to do. The good spirit that is moving him to the contrary causes him to be depressed in mind and moves him to at least express his belief that keeping slaves is inconsistent with the Christian religion. Although this declaration somewhat eases the feeling of malaise arising from his conflicted conscience, the Holy Spirit still disturbs him about not opting out of the whole business, whatever the consequences. In all this the evil spirit is supporting the movements (thoughts, feelings, inclinations) to avoid embarrassment even at the cost of violating his Christian conviction. Woolman fails to face down the evil spirit promptly and boldly, as Ignatius urges in rule I, 12.

In paragraph 2, the stressful situation he was in during his journey was an occasion for spiritual desolation: feelings of confusion, of lack of trust in God and of resignation to him. In his distress, he turned to God in prayer (rule I, 6) and, after a time, experienced spiritual consolation: resignation, calmness of mind, peaceful trust (rules I, 3, 7f.). Through the whole experience of temptation and desolation, God was showing Woolman his weakness, humbling him, and forming him (rule I, 9: *Commentary*, 182–91).

In paragraph 3 we see another experience of alternating spiritual desolation and consolation: a sense of being abandoned by God in his difficulties, deep distress of mind, and, after prayer to God for help, an awareness of spiritual consolation (rule I, 1–4, 6–8).

● *Response to Questions for Case 5* ●

1. According to rules I, 2, 4, and II, 1, it is connatural for the evil spirit to disturb, confuse, sadden, and discourage those who are spiritually maturing, to suggest misleading thoughts (arising from these disturbing feelings) and specious lines of reasoning. All these tactics of the evil spirit are evident in paragraph 2.

2. Rule I, 13, calls attention to the evil spirit's trick of suggesting reasons for keeping his disturbances and temptations hidden from any experienced and knowledgeable spiritual counselor and thus preventing the good results of openness with such a counselor. What is said in paragraph 3 illustrates the action of the evil spirit, and the developments in paragraphs 4 and 5 demonstrate the good results of opening up to a wise counselor.

In paragraph 5 there is also an indication that being open, sharing her inner life with anyone, was difficult for Lucia. Rule I, 14, explains that the evil spirit searches out where each one is especially vulnerable and attacks this person at that point.

   3. Rule I, 6, 12.

   4. Rule I, 7.

● *Response to Questions for Case 6* ●

   1. Rules I, 2, 14, and II, 1, 4f. In rule II, 1, Ignatius warns against the deceptions that Satan uses to harm those who have learned to withstand his direct and open attacks. The whole experience related here begins with what appears to be a good thought, one that could come to a person striving to become unselfish and guarding against any selfishness invading her spiritual life, a thought that appears to be in accord with her vocation as a wife and mother, a thought that could be taken to be inspired by the Holy Spirit. What follows in continuity with that thought, however, does not bear the marks of the Holy Spirit: not peace and joy, not spiritual courage and energy, but inability to read Sacred Scripture or to meditate, disturbance of mind, restlessness, distractions, harsh thoughts and feelings about the retreat director. All these consequences of the original good thought are signs of the evil spirit's influence and point to him as the prompting source of the thought with which the unsettling experience began (I, 2; II, 5).

   This thought was proposed in a way that appealed to Stella's loving, warm family life suggested in paragraph 1 of the case. The evil spirit found a healthy and good point in Stella that could serve as an opening for his deception (I, 14).

   2. Paragraphs 4 and 5 offer an interesting twist on Ignatius's rule I, 12, in which he urges us to confront the evil spirit boldly. Stella, without being aware of doing so, is letting the evil spirit manipulate her. It is her husband who sees what is going on, who boldly confronts the evil spirit, blunts the force of his influence, and opens Stella to the action of the Holy Spirit.

   3. In paragraph 6 of the case, Stella does what Ignatius in rule I, 13, counsels us to do, and by so doing she finds that the effect of the diabolical deceit has been nullified, replaced by the effects of the Holy Spirit on a maturing Christian.

● *Response to Case 7: The Author's Comments* ●

[As noted above at the end of the case, in place of questions and answers for reflection, the author's own reflections on his experience are given here. Each of the following numbered paragraphs corresponds to the paragraph of the same number in the preceding account of his experience. The words of the author are given below, with his references to the Ignatian rules in parentheses. See whether you find Kevin's reflections on his experience satisfactory or not. If not, why not? The author's comments begin with the following paragraph.]

I would see Kevin as predominantly a spiritually maturing person who is now being affected by the evil spirit. I believe Kevin is spiritually maturing, because he keeps returning to prayer even if at times he becomes tepid about it. I would further see the evil one causing him to regress in at least one area of his life (violating his marriage vow by engaging sexually with Jessica), but do not see this as a sign of a predominant life orientation away from God.

1.   Perhaps the evil one is affecting Kevin through his workaholism. Maybe Kevin's weak spot (I, 14) is his inability to say no or a feeling that he can take on the world. Perhaps these requests feed Kevin's ego. In any case, as we shall see in paragraph 2, they weaken him physically, emotionally, and spiritually.

2.   This is nonspiritual desolation. It is not yet involved in God with a direction away from faith, hope, and love (I, 4).

3.   I am assuming from the following paragraphs that Kevin is in spiritual desolation: he spends little time in personal prayer, he has grown tepid in his spiritual exercises. Further, I would see rule I, 13, operating here: he has all sorts of specious reasons not to see his spiritual director when he really does need to see her.

4.   A relationship of friendship with Jessica probably is or could be a real blessing in Kevin's life: he needs friends. But I believe rule I, 14, is operative here. Kevin is at an extremely vulnerable point in his life, and Satan goes in for the kill. Kevin gets involved sexually in violation of his marriage vow, seeing it as a gift of God and as prayer! It is a consolation from the evil spirit, a trap. Satan has appeared as an angel of light (II, 4f.).

5.   In the sinful dimension of his being, Kevin is experiencing the effects of the Holy Spirit, causing him to feel guilt and confusion. However, he talks about it neither to Jessica nor to a confessor; rather he finds many excuses for not doing so (I, 13).

6.   The experience in this paragraph is spiritual desolation. It is about Kevin's feelings toward God and is directing him away from faith, hope, and love. It is from the evil one, causing feelings of anger, gloom, confusion, and discouragement about his spiritual life (I, 4).

7.   Happily, he makes no quick decision while in spiritual desolation (I, 5). He seeks retreat, and insists more on prayer (I, 6).

8. His discouragement could be a nonspiritual or a spiritual desolation. He is discouraged in his prayer and this discouragement could be from the evil one.

9. This is spiritual consolation (I, 3; II, 1). It is God-centered with feelings of love, elation, and praise leading to a greater faith, hope, love with thanks and praise.

10. The evil one is putting up obstacles. What is of itself very beautiful causes a severe nonspiritual desolation, which is the occasion for his spiritual desolation. Kevin loses courage in face of temptation (I, 14). The devil knows where Kevin is most vulnerable (I, 14).

11. The experience related here is consolation, but it is a nonspiritual, deceptive consolation initiated by the evil one, leading Kevin to make a stupid and rash decision and end his prayer time before the two weeks is over. He was not testing the consolation (II, 4f.).

12. The Holy Spirit, initiating restlessness, awakens him from sleep (almost like the call of Samuel). The consolation is spiritual: feelings of God-centered peace, leading to following Christ dispossessed.

In light of the Ignatian rules, I would encourage Kevin to see how the evil one affected him during this period. It would be good for Kevin to know where he is especially vulnerable and to know that sometimes the devil can work through Kevin's tiredness when he tries to take on the world. Kevin will need to make some decisions regarding his own lifestyle, so that he can have more balance and time for prayer. It would also be good for him to seek out a spiritual director or talk over with his current director his own uncomfortableness with her approach. Finally, he needs to straighten out his relationship with Jessica.

●   *Responses to Questions for Case 8*   ●

1. In paragraph 1, the pertinent rules are I, 2; II, 7; and to some extent, I, 4. In I, 2, Ignatius says that it is connatural for the evil spirit to "thrust obstacles" in the way of those who are "ascending from good to better in the service of God our Lord." The one relating this experience seems to be such a person; and the restlessness, especially the inner debate of where and how to pray, are obstacles to actually praying. They constitute the "noise and disturbance" that rule II, 7, says the evil spirit effects in those who are disposed towards spiritual growth. Although all this, as the author of the case says, leads toward the confusion noted in rule I, 4, and does hinder prayer, the experience does not seem to be one of spiritual desolation: it does not of itself attack faith, hope, and charity. Not every movement prompted by or exacerbated by the evil spirit to hinder spiritual growth is spiritual

desolation. For their contrary purposes, both the Holy Spirit and the evil spirit prompt many movements other than spiritual consolation or desolation.

2. In paragraph 2, rules I, 2, 3, and 12, apply. The antispiritual movements from the evil spirit should be opposed with a "bold front" (rule I, 12). This is what the affected person did by recognizing what was happening, breaking off the inner debate, and praying against it. The prompting to do this is from the Holy Spirit, as also are the consequences: "a quiet mind . . . ease of action, and taking away obstacles for the sake of progress in doing good" (rule I, 2). Along with these effects, the prayer that followed was touched with spiritual consolation, which in accord with rule I, 3, is spoken of as "peaceful," with "a strong sense of the Lord's loving acceptance and transforming power."

● *Response to Questions for Case 9* ●

1. Both rules I, 1 and 2, apply. In one dimension of his personality, Augustine is firmly disposed towards sin and is affected by the evil spirit in accord with that disposition. As a consequence, he dreaded giving up his "customary indulgence" and drew back from the inclination to give over his life to God. In another dimension of his personality, the Holy Spirit is touching Augustine's deep disposition toward knowing truth and living in accord with it. As a consequence, he experiences shame and confusion at his cowardly and sinful way of life.

2. Yes, rule II, 7, clarifies the rules I, 1f. Rules I, 3f., give fuller descriptions of how the good and evil spirits affect the dimension of a person who is disposed in accord with the Holy Spirit. Rules I, 4 and 12, also illuminate Augustine's experiences. The evil spirit attacks him in his weakest point. His failure boldly to oppose the evil spirit prolonged the evil spirit's increasingly fierce attack (see *Confessions,* bks. 8–11.)

● *Responses to Questions for Case 10* ●

1. Given what was said above about Joanna, all these negative feelings are most probably nonspiritual, merely her psychological reaction to the prospect of being in an unusual setting with a group of strangers whose ways of thinking and mode of worship she expects to be far different from her own.

2. Again, very likely nonspiritual movements but with positive feelings.

3. This is clearly consolation, but whether only aesthetic or truly spiritual is unclear without further data.

4. While praise and thanks to God are spiritual movements, they do not necessarily involve spiritual consolation. However, in context, it seems almost certain that Joanna is experiencing consolation and most likely that the consolation is a spiritual one.

5. Now, there can be no doubt that Joanna is experiencing a spiritual consolation, one rooted in living faith.

6. Joanna is experiencing spiritual desolation. The decisive factor is her inclination to doubt God's love. Without that, what is described could be a nonspiritual desolation.

7. This is spiritual consolation: there is a feeling of peace and tranquil joy rooted in living faith.

8. Joanna could be having spiritual desolation or spiritual consolation, depending on whether or not she trusts God's power to enable her to grow into truly Christian love and humility. As the statement stands, we are uncertain.

9. This looks like a spiritual desolation, occasioned perhaps by Joanna's emotional instability. Without more information one could make a case that the whole experience is only nonspiritual desolation, a letdown after the intense emotional experience of the preceding evening.

10. Up to the point of saying that Joanna "sees herself as ugly and unlovable," we have the subjective grounds for a desolation. From there on, it becomes clear that the desolation which arises from these grounds is a spiritual desolation, one that directly, of itself, attacks her living faith.

11. This is clearly a spiritual consolation, one rooted in living faith.

●   *Responses to Questions for Case 11*   ●

1. In paragraph 1, the pianist's whole manner and in particular her spontaneous refrain of "Praise God" suggest that she meant what she was singing. If so, then surely she was expressing lively faith, humility, and thanksgiving to God as all these are expressed in the hymn she was singing. No such faith is possible without the action of the Holy Spirit here and now. Nothing in the paragraph explicitly indicates a spiritual movement taking place in Kerr; but his attitude and his "Thank you" to the singer, along with the whole context, suggest that he was experiencing along with the singer her sentiments rooted in faith and love and was also, therefore, being moved by the Holy Spirit. While the term spiritual consolation is not employed and while such consolation is not necessarily experienced with acts of faith, thanks, and praise, spiritual consolation in both these persons seems to be implied by the tone of the author's account.

2. In paragraph 2 Kerr's response to the family with the spastic daughter and her fall could be understood as possibly an experience of admirable tender but nonspiritual compassion, until we find him moved to pray to Jesus for the girl and to reflect on Jesus' own fall on the way of the cross and his need of help. These movements flow from his Christian faith and so, ultimately, from the Holy Spirit. Again, implicitly and almost certainly, spiritual consolation is implied.

3. Here also, in paragraph 3, all Kerr says could be understood as a deep emotional response, expressed with touching eloquence, to an instance of beautiful filial piety—until it all relates in his mind and heart with the divine exhortation to "honor your father." At this point it is clear that his thought and feeling are rooted in living faith, are spiritual.

4. Yes, assuming that by theophany is meant (as Kerr seems to mean) any experienced manifestation of God acting in our lives. If the criteria that Ignatius gives for discerning when our thoughts and affections are prompted by the Holy Spirit are valid, then we can tell when the spirit is acting on our minds and hearts, revealing his loving concern and giving us guidance. In the responses to questions 1 to 3, reasons, based on Ignatian teaching, have been given for thinking that this was happening in the three episodes which Kerr recounts.

● *Responses to Questions for Case 12* ●

1. It looks very much as though Jim has an emotional problem, an authority hang-up, and needs psychological therapy. He blames himself for his emotional response to authority figures as if it were a moral failure for which he is responsible and could overcome just by goodwill. As a consequence (and prompted by the "father of lies") he falls into spiritual desolation.

2. Given Jim's psychological problem with authority, it is understandable that he would seek help from someone other than an authority figure. His choice, however, is unwise to begin with and, as it turns out, harmful. In rule I, 13, Ignatius does not recommend opening one's spiritual life to just any well-meaning person, but to a counselor who is spiritually experienced, knowledgeable, and wise. There was no reason to think that George had these qualities, and his well-meaning attempt to help Jim proved that he did not. He had no understanding of the difference between a spiritual, a moral, and a purely psychological problem or of the different basic kinds of therapy that each case calls for (though each kind of therapy can be helpful to the others when they are wisely carried out in conjunction).

3. This compulsive decision is made in violation of rule I, 5. Even if by chance what he decided and carried out is the same decision that

would rightly be made in suitable circumstances and with sound method, the time and way of making it are wrong. The risk of acting in discord with the Holy Spirit is too great, and the person acting on such a decision will likely find himself uncertain and regretful later on.

4. As it is described, Jim's feeling of satisfaction in his decision has nothing about it to suggest a spiritual consolation. His negative feelings, as stated, have no marks of a spiritual desolation. Even if he were experiencing a spiritual consolation and a spiritual desolation, these would not indicate that his decision has been a right one or a wrong one. If Jim's conflicting feelings were spiritual consolation and spiritual desolation and if they were a confirmation and a disconfirmation of his decision, his confusion would be understandable; but being contrary nonspiritual responses to different events, his contrary feelings offer no ground for any confusion and certainly have no bearing on the value of Ignatian discernment.

5. Euphoria is consolation, but not necessarily spiritual consolation. Gratitude to God is a spiritual experience but not necessarily a consolation. Jim might be experiencing spiritual consolation, but what is said in paragraph 5 gives no convincing evidence for thinking so.

• *Responses to Questions for Case 13* •

1. Everything described in paragraphs 1 to 11 shows the influence of the Holy Spirit acting on both the spiritually good and the spiritually bad dimensions of De Lorean's personality. Rules II, 7, and I, 2 and 4, cast light on what is going on.

De Lorean's desire to understand what was happening in his life and to read the Bible as a help to this understanding, his constant impulse to meditate on the Bible, his realization that his former values were questionable, his inclination to pray, his readiness to listen to the seminarian prison guard, his insight into God's love and the meaning of Christ in his life, his insight into his false idea of himself as captain of his fate, in charge of his own life, gaining salvation by his own efforts alone, his willingness to give over control of his life to God—all these movements are effects of the Holy Spirit touching on the good dimension of his personality, the one in harmony with the Holy Spirit.

The Holy Spirit is also touching on the contrary dimension of De Lorean's personality, where he has deep-seated egoistic dispositions in discord with the Holy Spirit. The consequent effects of the Holy Spirit are disturbing to him: confusion, a sense that there is something very wrong with his values and his way of living, consequent feelings of anger, frustration, and fear, seeing himself as an "ego maniac," a "living lie," and finally feeling himself a broken man, struck down.

2. The consequent openness to God prepared him for the gift of overpowering spiritual consolation (rule I, 3), perhaps even a consolation without previous cause (rule II, 2), an experience that exceeded any spiritual consolation that could be expected to follow from his new understanding of himself and his new relationship to God. Without more information, however, we could not be sure.

3. If the consolation described in paragraph 13 was a consolation without previous cause, then what De Lorean describes in paragraph 14 seems to be an afterglow of the spiritual consolation properly speaking. The actual consolation that he refers to as a divine "embrace" had ended and now he is "again alone in my cell, yet not alone"—alone in the sense that the presence and embrace of God experienced just before had ended, even though he still felt the deep reverberations of that experience. However, a careful reading of paragraphs 14 and 15 suggests that De Lorean was now also experiencing an actual consolation with previous cause, a consolation that flows from his heightened understanding of how much he is loved by God.

● *Responses to Questions for Case 14* ●

1. In the "thick darkness," the "fog," that surrounds and penetrates Thérèse, the Christian image of her fatherland, of heaven, is obscured, and her Christian faith in its reality is attacked and consequently her hope of coming to it (see especially paragraph 3). Any desolation that of itself tends to weaken and ultimately destroy a living faith is a spiritual desolation.

2. There is no reason to question whether one can have undiminished acts of living faith during spiritual desolation. Actual diminishment of faith, hope, and charity is not a necessary factor in the experience of spiritual desolation. A tendency toward diminishment is so; but this tendency may never cause any actual diminishment of the essential acts of faith, hope, and charity. The experience of spiritual desolation might even be an occasion for growth in purity and intensity of living faith in the person who endures and resists spiritual desolation with "courage and energy." (See below, response to question 4.)

3. Not only can one have living faith even with increased intensity and purity without experiencing spiritual consolation, one can even at a deeper, more inward dimension or level of conscious life experience a spiritual consolation resulting from one's enduring spiritual desolation with faithful love in union with Christ's salvific suffering. This is clearly what Thérèse is describing in paragraphs 1 and 6 of her account.

4. Thérèse's experience makes even clearer and more explicit than Ignatius does in rule I, 9, that God might allow spiritual desolation in

order to purify one's Christian hope for heaven of any merely natural, self-centered motivation.

It may be worth noting that, although Thérèse was a great mystic, the experience she relates in the whole passage under study here does not exhibit the features of the passive dark night of the spirit which John of the Cross describes and to which the Ignatian rules do not apply. (See *Commentary*, 271–82, especially 278f.).

•   *Response to Question for Case 15*   •

In paragraph 2, from what is said there it is not clear whether Adele's restlessness and inner confusion are a spiritual or a nonspiritual movement. Her desire to spend more time in prayer and the accompanying thought that God might be calling her to the contemplative way of life (meaning, I assume, a cloistered, purely contemplative way), all this is as yet of uncertain origin. It would be necessary first of all to find out whether the desire and thought were integral with spiritual consolation. If they were, then the whole experience was probably from the Holy Spirit; but it would have to be tested to make sure it was not a deception of the evil spirit such as Ignatius describes in rules II, 3–5.

3. Adele is clearly falling into the trap mentioned in rule I, 13. She is moved by the evil spirit or at least plays into his hands.

4, 5. Adele moves in the right direction by seeking counsel; but, as she became aware only afterwards, the counselor she chose was not, as rule I, 13, recommends, someone skilled in discernment of spirits. However, as it turned out, the counselor she chose could and did supply the psychological therapy Adele needed, so we may believe the Holy Spirit led her to him. His suggestion that Adele not attempt a decision about a change to contemplative life until she reached a healthier emotional condition seems sound; for otherwise she would neither have the tranquility needed for discerning God's will nor have sufficient data.

6. Now the influence of the evil spirit as described in rule I, 4, becomes evident. Adele experiences a direct attack on her faith life: discouragement, inability to pray, and, most significantly, a sense of God's absence, the thought that God doesn't care about her or her future. In this situation, the rules would urge Adele to confront the evil spirit promptly and boldly (I, 12) and strongly counterattack (I, 6) with patience and confidence that consolation will soon return (I, 8) and that meanwhile, with God's always available help, she can overcome all obstacles (I, 7). Further, rule I, 13, advises that she defeat the evil spirit's deception and temptation by conferring with someone who is skilled in discernment of spirits. Instead of acting in accord with these counsels, Adele keeps her own counsel about her spiritual life and

allows her attention to it to fade away. Nevertheless, throughout Adele's desolation the Holy Spirit was still active in keeping her faith, hope, and charity alive. This is evidently true because her desolation was a spiritual one. Any who never had or have entirely lost their living faith could not experience what Ignatius calls a spiritual desolation.

7. Despite Adele's pusillanimous response to the evil spirit's attack, the Holy Spirit with loving kindness not only sustains her living faith but also gives her relief and spiritual consolation from time to time, as Ignatius assures her will happen (I, 8). Rule I, 10, counsels a reflective and prayerful preparation during these times of consolation in order to meet the expected return of desolation. There is no evidence that Adele did this.

8. Here we see that even during desolation the Holy Spirit moved Adele to at least one mode of counterattacking, by appropriate spiritual reading, and this occasioned a return of spiritual consolation, even unusually deep consolation. This experience confirms that the desolation was spiritual and that Ignatius's emphasis on counterattacking is wise, not because we can by our own efforts attain spiritual consolation, but because God rewards our efforts by freely giving the gift.

9. Any inclination to change, during spiritual desolation, a previously well-made decision with which she had been at peace was wisely seen as a temptation of the evil spirit (I, 5). Remaining firm in her previous decision to attend summer school is wise, as also the choice of courses to help her carry out a serious discernment of God's will regarding her future.

10, 11. Leaving aside what might be said about Adele's dispositions for and process of discerning God's will, the spiritual movements she experiences occur in striking contrast, spiritual peace (I, 3) giving way to an unmistakable and deep spiritual desolation, with all the symptoms described in rule I, 4.

12. The practical value of studying the Ignatian rules shows up clearly now. Adele does what she failed to do in her previous desolation. (See above, comment on paragraph 6.)

13. Here the good results of acting in accord with rule I, 13, and other rules during the time of desolation are evident: rational clarity, calm, intensified faith, hope, and charity, with peace.

● *Response to the Question for Case 16* ●

[The paragraph numbers in this response correspond with the paragraph numbers in the case itself.]

1. What is said in this paragraph suggests that Dorothy fits predominantly under rule I, 2. She is concerned with purging away her sins and ascending from good to better in God's service by good works, by fidelity and prayer.

2. This judgment about Dorothy as dominantly a maturing Christian is confirmed by her sincere repentance when she fails and also by the spiritual consolation that she derives from the sacrament, along with the inspiration she experiences to continue her good works.

3. Here we see the evil spirit attacking Dorothy at her weak point, her negative feelings of anger and so on toward others (I, 14). These feelings toward others become an occasion for negative feelings about herself. These feelings, in turn, constitute a desolation, whether spiritual or nonspiritual is not clear. But in any case Dorothy is impelled to act in discord with rule I, 5, by deciding to cease visiting the sick and elderly. On the other hand, the influence of the Holy Spirit is evident in her trusting prayer and her sacramental confession—to say nothing of her living faith, which makes it possible for her to experience the kind of desolation she does over her unchristian feelings.

4. This time Dorothy's desolation is clearly spiritual, attacking her faith in God's forgiving love (I, 4). Again, and more clearly and seriously in conflict with rule I, 5, she makes a harmful decision while in spiritual desolation, the decision to withdraw from participation in the Eucharist.

5. Even though Dorothy did not seek help from Sister Angela, she was open to receive it (I, 13). Her consolation (her feelings of happiness and tears of joy) seems to be nonspiritual, a natural, human response to a feeling of being loved, to an awareness that someone is concerned about her. However that may be, Sister Angela is the instrument of God to help Dorothy escape the deceptions of the evil spirit and find peace.

● *Response to Questions for Case 17* ●

1. Marietta's anger and desire to kill the one who had caused such terrible pain to those she loves was a natural, spontaneous emotional reaction but very likely encouraged by the evil spirit, with the intention of leading her to a free and sinful act of hatred. Obviously, Marietta was in a terrible desolation, but not what Ignatius names spiritual desolation. Overcoming her anger and spontaneous desire to kill the kidnapper and, in accord with God's will, to love and forgive the kidnapper—all this was clearly, as Marietta understood it to be (see paragraphs 1 and 4 in the account of her experience), the work of the Holy Spirit in her. (See rules I, 2 and 12.)

2. Using Marietta's nonspiritual desolation as an occasion, the evil spirit suggests a line of thought that leads to spiritual desolation, involving a direct attack on Marietta's faith life.

3. A loving response of the Holy Spirit in this situation was to strengthen Marietta by an intense spiritual consolation, one that might even have been what Ignatius means by a consolation without previous cause (see rule II, 2).

4. It is highly unlikely that at first Marietta's love for and forgiveness of Susie's murderer involved *feelings* of love. In fact, her feelings could still be those of anger and hate. Most likely she was experiencing what Ignatius, in rule I, 2, speaks of as "courage and spiritual energy" to elicit by free choice an *act* of love without loving feelings. But it becomes clear that the Holy Spirit finally moves Marietta to a more complete response of compassionate love for a mentally sick brother in Christ, a love that included tender feelings. Here we see the amazing triumph of the Holy Spirit in Marietta over her temptation to anger and a desire to kill, her temptation to doubt the reality of God and his love. This victory is all the more clearly a work of the Holy Spirit in her because of the natural and diabolical promptings to the contrary. At this time Marietta is aware of the intensification of her faith and purification of her love into a more Christlike love. Consequently, she would be experiencing genuine *spiritual* consolation, along with, no doubt, a continuing nonspiritual desolation over the tragedy of Susie's death and the suffering of her family.

● *Response to Questions for Case 18* ●

1. What is said in paragraph 1 of the case seems to indicate someone who is predominantly a maturing Christian (I, 2).

2. Rose Ellen's hurt and anger are understandable spontaneous emotional reactions to being fired—unjustly, as she saw the event; no prompting from the evil spirit need be supposed to understand them. What follows, however, shows the influence of the evil spirit: her unforgiving attitude, the irrational and unjust extension of her bitter anger to all priests, to the Church, and even to God; her experience of spiritual desolation; her decision to turn away from prayer and to discontinue her work in God's service (rules I, 2, 4, 5).

3. As emphasized more than once already, none of us is purely the kind of person spoken of in rules I, 1 and 2. In what way or ways Rose Ellen is a rule-1 person appears in paragraph 2. No doubt much can be said to make understandable her reactions to what seems to her, and perhaps was, a serious and demeaning injustice. However, without further information, we know nothing of her boss's reason for firing her

and so do not know whether Rose Ellen's judgment of the event is true. Even if her judgment of the event should turn out to be true, her response to it reveals seriously unchristian dispositions. It also suggests strong influence of the evil spirit, who would surely be trying to intensify her negative feelings and her judgments flowing from them. (See rule I, 4, the last part.) There is no evidence of openness to the Holy Spirit, who would be prompting her to Christian trust in God, humility, and forgiveness. The readiness with which she allows her bitterness to extend to the clergy in general and beyond them to the Church and even to God betrays a tragic psychological and spiritual immaturity. The collapse of her relationship with God in this situation betrays the frailty of her faith, hope, and charity.

In direct response, then, to question 3, I find my response to paragraph 1 severely shaken. I am left wondering how much of what appeared as growing in Christian maturity before she was put to the test was really covering up subtle egoism, and how much Rose Ellen is in truth predominantly a rule-1 person, a person with strong basic dispositions in opposition to the Holy Spirit.

4. Yes. First of all she should have opened herself to someone experienced in and learned about discernment of spirits (I, 13). She needed to reflect on the signs of the good and evil spirits as in rules I, 1–4. She needed to understand and observe the counsel given in rule I, 5, about not changing decisions when in spiritual desolation and the counsels in rule I, 6–8 and 12, about patiently and confidently counterattacking spiritual desolation and temptation.

5. For those who believe in God's providence over our lives, making all work out for God's greater glory in us, it is easy to see why God would permit Rose Ellen to experience what is recounted in paragraph 2, in order to prepare her for the work to be undertaken later on, which is described in paragraph 3.

● *Response to Question for Case 19* ●

1. The thoughts that horrify Sadie could be seen as merely a surprising psychological event. However, the way they affect Sadie's life gives strong reason for judging that they are the work of an evil spirit, at least in the broad sense of that term, and very likely of an evil spirit in the proper sense, causing or taking advantage of the situation. The whole experience fits with Ignatius's description, in rules I, 2 and 4, and in rule II, 1, of the feelings and diabolical deceptions. As a consequence of her "dreadful faults," Sadie is led to think that she is one of the most wicked of sinners and that she had never really been a good Christian. This way of thinking causes a deep spiritual desolation: confusion,

darkness, discouragement, sense of separation from God. The whole experience is a tissue of lies and feelings that are characteristics of Satan's influence on a maturing Christian, all intended to hinder her growth in living faith and even turn her away from even trying at all to lead a Christlike life.

Sadie could be given helpful counsel based on many of the rules. She needs enlightenment from one who understands the tricks of the evil spirit (I, 13) and can support her to be bold and confident in rejecting the evil spirit's lies (I, 12), patiently and perseveringly to go contrary to any discouraging inclination by acts of faith in God's love, and to meditate on Scripture texts that assure her of God's love (I, 6–8). She needs to reflect on why God allows this painful experience (I, 9), in order to see how her experience can be an occasion for her growth towards spiritual maturity (toward humility, trust, patience, understanding of and compassion for others when they are enduring temptation and desolation). When the evil spirit sees that attacking her in the way he does only occasions her spiritual growth, he will back off and try some other trick, perhaps one of the deceptions that Ignatius explains in rules II. Time enough to explain these rules when she needs them.

● ***Response to Questions for Case 20*** ●

1. From what is said in this case, Alice appears to be predominantly the maturing Christian of rule I, 2, but having in some dimension of her personality dispositions in discord with the evil spirit.

2. One of Alice's weak points seems to be the vice associated with her virtue of enthusiasm and drive. She is impatient to get successful results and impatient with those who do not move with her; she cannot cope well with failure. Without formulating her thought, she tends to see success in her projects as a sign of God's loving care and failure as a sign of God's rejection. The evil spirit has spotted this weak point and worked on it so as to lead her into a spiritual desolation (I, 2, 4, 14). Under the influence of spiritual desolation, she changes what before seemed to be a sound decision (I, 5).

3. Rule I, 12 and 6, along with 7f., would help to change for the better her whole attitude toward desolation and the events that ground it. Rule I, 9, would assist this change and enable her to cooperate with what God is doing for her by allowing the failure of her efforts and her painful desolation as well. Rule I, 5, would warn her away from her untimely decision to withdraw from her efforts to enliven her parish. A study and application or rules II, 3–5, might uncover the deception described in those rules.

• **Response to Question for Case 21** •

[The numbers correspond with the numbers in the case.]

1. Susan's purpose, in accord with the aim of the Ignatian rules, is rooted in faith and seems to be prompted by the Holy Spirit.

2. These months are characterized by movements of the good spirit: "courage and active energy, consolations, . . . a quiet mind, giving ease of action and taking away obstacles for the sake of progress in doing good" (Rule I, 2). The significance of her welcoming appreciative remarks about her work will appear in later paragraphs.

3. The action of the Holy Spirit shows in the strengthening of Susan's faith through her seeing retreatants touched by the power of the Gospel. On the other hand, because she was weighed down by responsibilities and stressed by the "hectic pace" of work, her sense of the spirit's presence in her own prayer diminished. The evil spirit seems to be using her success in ministry to draw her from needed prayer (II, 4). She does not yet seem to be in spiritual desolation: her experience of dryness does not yet directly affect her faith life. It seems rather to be an occasion for the spiritual desolation that will appear in paragraphs 4 and 5 of her account.

4–5. Now spiritual desolation appears: confusion and discouragement about her life of faith, hope, and love (I, 4), a clear sign of the evil spirit at work. Perhaps Susan undertakes too much work either because she is driven by the bad motive of wanting to be important or because she is deceived by the evil spirit (II, 4f.). Another sign of the influence of the evil spirit now shows up: She hides from her spiritual director her problem with prayer and her spiritual desolation and talks only about her apparently successful ministry (I, 13). The desire, which Susan mentions further on, of maintaining a "superwoman image" makes her an easy victim for this evil spirit's deception (I, 14). As a consequence, she receives no guidance on how to counterattack (I, 6) or any encouraging reminders, such as those Ignatius gives in rules I, 7f. and 11, or any enlightenment on why God permits the desolation (I, 9) and what part she had in bringing it on. As a result, Susan falls more deeply into the trap laid for her, indiscreetly taking on more and more activity to the detriment of prayer and spiritual tranquility, finding more and more self-satisfaction in appearing to be the generous and successful superwoman in God's service, losing touch with God, and falling into deeper spiritual desolation. True enough, God does sometimes call persons to heroic labors that would destroy others, but Susan is clearly not one of these.

6. The reversal of all that had been going on when, during the Spiritual Exercises, Susan let go of her superwoman image and began

living within her limits, confirms the preceding interpretation of what was going on and shows the activity of the Holy Spirit in bringing about her healing.

● *Response to the Question for Case 22* ●

[The following application of the Ignatian rules to the events of each day is that given by the author of this case, just as she gave it, with a few minor editorial changes.]

Day 1: Jane is a spiritually maturing person, ascending from good to better; the good spirit is bringing a quiet mind for the sake of progress in good (I, 2).

Day 2: Jane is receiving spiritual consolation, an inward gladness attracting her to heavenly things, bringing her repose and peace in the Lord (I, 3). The spiritual director could have profitably cautioned her that the consolation will not last and that she needs to prepare for desolation (I, 10).

Day 3: Jane is experiencing a spiritual consolation with a preceding cause, an experience that seems good at first but soon begins to exhibit signs of the evil spirit: imprudent resolution to prolong prayer, high excitement, inability to fall asleep (II, 3–5). Jane plays into the hands of the evil spirit by not being sufficiently open with her spiritual director (I, 13). The latter, knowing her volatile emotional temperament, would most likely have (and certainly should have) dissuaded her from prolonging her prayer. The spiritual director could have advised her to humble and lower herself after yesterday's consolation rather than to try to prolong or repeat it (I, 11).

Days 4–5: Jane's mood here is a nonspiritual desolation that still hinders her prayer (I, 2). It is good that she told her director, for this exposed to light the enemy's trickery (I, 13). It is possible now to see the entire process as the work of the evil spirit: the good thoughts ended up in spiritual desolation and distracted her from the purpose of her retreat by weakening her (II, 4f.). She should be helped to look back at the whole course of the experience (days 3 to 5) to see how the thoughts began (desire for consolation, decision to prolong prayer) and how the evil spirit used them to destroy her peace (II, 6). She should also be made aware of her weaknesses: her excitability and rapid undulation of moods, and her lack of balance (prolonging prayer). The evil spirit attacks us in our weaker areas (I, 14).

Day 6: Jane's desolation becomes a spiritual one, tending toward distrust, making her feel as if separated from God (I, 4). She should be encouraged to change her way and resist the evil spirit; but because of her disposition, it would not be wise to follow the suggestions in rule 6 to increase prayer, examination, penance (I, 6). The suggestions, however, given in some following rules (I, 7, 8, 11) are applicable—with special emphasis on trusting in God's loving power, which is sufficient to see her through all her trials. She should put up a bold front and hope against hope in the faithful love of God (I, 12). She should consider why God might be allowing this spiritual desolation and so be better able to respond to it (I, 9). Note that the evil spirit has taken advantage of another weak spot in Jane's personality, her tendency to discouragement and to feeling unworthy of being loved. (See the introduction to this case, in brackets.)

Days 7–8: The good spirit is now giving Jane a quiet mind and courage, pointing the way to overcome obstacles in doing good (I, 2). As rule I, 8, would assure her would happen, spiritual consolation does return.

●   *Response to Questions for Case 23*   ●

1. In paragraphs 1 and 2, there is no patent sign of the evil spirit. Kathy's severe nervousness is not surprising; it seems to be merely a falling back into her normal self-doubt and fear of failure. It would be reasonable, however, to think that the evil spirit would be aware of Kathy's weak point (I, 14) and would be working on it to hinder the good she was doing.

2. Kathy's connatural fear before giving a talk does put an obstacle in the way of her trust in God's providential care and of her prayer at the time. The unusual and unfounded intensity of it could suggest the influence of the evil spirit. It does cause some confusion and could be an obstacle to a good work for God. I would, then, certainly call it a temptation; but I would be less certain about whether it should be seen as a spiritual desolation—though what follows in paragraph 4 suggests that spiritual desolation is even now beginning. The important thing to note at the moment is that there is some force at work opposed to Christian faith and that the Holy Spirit is moving Kathy to see it for what it is and to take prayerful action against it.

3. In paragraph 4, Kathy's experience does seem to be spiritual desolation, bringing on two temptations with which Ignatius deals in the rules. The first temptation is, during a period of desolation, to change a well-made decision (I, 5) on which Kathy had acted for years with excellent results for the glory of God. The second temptation, to which Kathy for the moment succumbs, is to avoid opening up her experience to someone who is knowledgeable about the devices of the evil spirit (I, 13).

4. Rules I, 3, 8, 9 and 13, apply here. As Ignatius, in rule I, 8, says ordinarily happens, Kathy does soon experience relief from desolation and receives the gift of spiritual consolation (I, 8), deep peace and joy, courage and energy, all rooted in an ardent faith, along with blessings on her work.

●   *Response to Questions for Case 24*   ●

1. In answer to Stan's first question, the rules could assure him that the Lord is in the midst of "all this," always lovingly and powerfully present even when he seems to leave Stan on his own and not give him the consolation he had experienced before now (I, 7). What he is experiencing is spiritual desolation, sadness over the seeming absence of God, confusion, discouragement about his spiritual life (I, 4). The prompting source of this experience is the evil spirit (I, 2 and 5). However, spiritual desolation is possible only in a person who has faith in and love for God and only in proportion to that faith and love. For only such a one is saddened and confused and feels discouraged by the seeming absence of God and dryness in prayer. But faith in and love for God are sure signs that the Holy Spirit is lovingly present and working in Stan, preserving him in fundamental fidelity to his vocation. In the Spirit's power given to him, he can, promptly and boldly, diametrically oppose the influence of the evil spirit (I, 12) and overcome all obstacles to growth and union with God (I, 7). The thought that God has in reality left Stan alone when he is in desolation and is with him only when he feels the sweetness and comfort of the spirit's presence is a disastrous error, a lie that the father of lies uses time and again to deceive and discourage those who are striving to serve God.

2. The answer to Stan's second question is suggested in rule I, 9. There is a possibility that Stan has been negligent in skipping prayer times in favor of work. Whether or not he is at fault is not clear, but some questioning about this is called for. If Stan is at fault, it could be that God allows his desolation in order to make him aware of the danger to his life of union with God and to bring him back to fidelity in prayer. If he is not at fault, he can be sure that God is allowing his desolation for his spiritual growth in one or both of two ways. First, he is teaching Stan to know experientially that he is unable to achieve spiritual consolation by his own effort, that this is God's gift; by so doing God is protecting him from vain glory when he does have consolation and helping him grow in humility. Secondly, by allowing spiritual desolation to afflict Stan and at the same time giving him the grace to be faithful and trusting while enduring and resisting the desolation, God is enabling Stan to grow in faith, hope, and love in a way that would have been impossible for him amidst spiritual consolation.

3. Stan's third question, whether he should seek to withdraw from his position as vocation director, is for the moment answered by rule I, 5. There Ignatius tells us that since spiritual desolation is prompted by the evil spirit (only allowed by God), we should strongly suspect that the plans and attractions arising from the desolation are also prompted by the evil spirit. If the question still appears to be a reasonable one after Stan has been restored to spiritual consolation or at least a state of spiritual calm, he can make a serious discernment of God's will in the matter and trust that decision.